Message from the Ancient Ones...

You are the seed of the new being. You are not the fruit — it is not time for you to decay — it's time for you to blossom. You can do more than you know. The ancestors will work with you and through you. Do not doubt yourself or them. We have waited a long time for you to be ready. There are others too, coming of age. All of Creation is supporting you. The ground is ready — the ground of consciousness. Your fertile ground is in consciousness — be the gardener in consciousness.

Looking west from Trousers Point Coastal Track
Flinders Island, Tasmania

Praise for *Ancient Ones Are Calling Us*

"In *Ancient Ones Are Calling Us*, Sue Cimino tells her beguiling and meaningful story of awakening. I was entranced from the beginning with the open, honest rendition of her journey and with her invitation to us to join together in community and consciousness. The book is a must read for all who truly care about awareness and our future. This work is important. Don't miss it!"

> ~ **Elsie Ritzenhein,** author of *Awakening Your Creative Voice/Women in a World of Possibility* (2017) and Creative Director/CEO of Inspiring Creative Women, LLC, elsieritzenhein.com

"Sue's book is captivating, motivating and inspirational. Her unlikely progression from accountant to spiritual conduit is fascinating and deeply revelatory. Her written expression flows effortlessly and wraps you in suspense and wonder. Wonder at her gifts as well as the unfoldment of the readers' gifts. A book that you don't want to end – even when the pages stop – you know the story is never ending."

> ~ **Noel K. Marshall, PhD,** Co-founder: LightPartners.org, Co-Founder: CoCreatorsConvergence.com

"*Ancient Ones are Calling Us* by Sue Cimino is a wonderfully written book that carries an essential message for our world. Sue's lighthearted description of her journey to connecting with and completely trusting her inner guidance is an inspiration for us all. Sue is a wonderfully heart-centered individual whose guidance has opened my eyes to my divine purpose in a way that totally changed my life. Read this book and let it transform your life."

> ~ **Ted Murray** - Author, *Tennis from the Heart-Pursuing the Dream*

"I love the tone and the tempo of this book. And most of all, Sue Cimino's message to all of us. The story feels true to me – very believable, and beautiful. Reading this story of opening up to your true meaning was inspiring in a very calming way. Cimino does not force-feed action points, she lets you follow the light and find your own path."

> ~ **Sinclair Lappi,** Author of the upcoming novel *Indigo Twin*

"Sue Cimino's book, *Ancient Ones Are Calling Us,* activates you to connect with your soul. While reading her story, **you are empowered to release the blocks to your spiritual essence.** Do yourself a favor and read this book!"

> ~ **Kathy Mason,** Author, speaker and trainer, <u>Masonworks Marketing.com</u>

"This book is terrific. Sue's experiences are profound and exciting. I felt very much inspired throughout. I was totally engaged and laughed out loud many times. I could see so much of myself in her story and feel you will too."

> ~ **Shulé Marie Besher,** Facilitator of Mystical Egypt Activation Tours

"Sue Cimino's gripping narrative of her remarkable adventures with the indigenous ancestors of Tasmania will enlighten and energize you for your own soul's calling. Following her journey from a successful career as an accountant as she becomes an adventurer into remote areas of Tasmania, she frankly and engagingly details the detours, the rocks in the road, and the doubts, as well as the inspiring high points and the timely companions who helped along the way and always must accompany us as we dare to live our lives to their most grand, full purpose."

> ~ **Trish Broersma,** Author, *Riding Into Your Mythic Life: Transformational Adventures with the Horse*

"Reading Cimino's writing is a peculiarly intimate experience: it's more than just being in the room listening to someone tell a fascinating story. Instead she engages the reader until they feel they're there, that they are living the narrator's experience. She has a wonderful, conversational easy-to-read voice that will transport you to far places and strange experiences. Take this journey of discovery with her!"

> ~ **Dave Freer,** Wall Street Journal best-seller listed author of 21 novels, including the Dragon Award shortlisted *Changeling's Island*

"A delightful and thought provoking tale describes Sue's unfolding life path from a logical accountant to a cosmic world adventurer. She travels to Tasmania and interfaces with aborigines, considered to be the oldest people on the planet to obtain a deep and ancient knowing that humanity is on the verge of a tremendous quantum leap. She encourages us to overcome our fear of fear to discover and embrace our uniquely beautiful self and live our unfolding soul's purpose, so we can play our role as one of the pattern-breakers within humanity in this new era. Lastly, she reminds us to be patient, continue to listen, hear, and celebrate ourselves as we discover what is possible."

> ~ **Lisa Tully, PhD,** Founder - Energy Medicine Research Institute, energymedicineri.com

"Sue Cimino's writing moves at an easy pace that makes her book a page-turner: *What's going to happen next?* She demonstrates a breadth of experience in the common or earthly world, as well as a familiarity with inner world. She does it in a way that is instructive—you can learn from her experiences. Artistic, heartful, and useful, a very good combination!"

> ~ **David Tresemer, PhD,** President, Association for Anthroposophic Psychology, AnthroposophicPsycho logy.org; Editor and contributor, *The Counselor...As If Soul and Spirit Matter*

"I felt as if I was walking hand and hand with Sue on her journey...my inner-knowing was reassured igniting my heart and soul."

> ~ **JoAnne Palladino,** Lightworker and Channel for Shmaya, the Beings of Light, joannepalladino.com

Ancient Ones Are Calling Us

Ancient Ones Are Calling Us

Learning to Listen Changed My Life

Sue Cimino

Sojourn Publishing, LLC

Image credits – Cover image by frank mckenna on
Unsplash.com
– All others by Sue Cimino

To contact the author:
www.SueCimino.com
Facebook – Sue Cimino – Author

Printed in the United States of America

First Printing, 2018

ISBN: 978-1-62747-211-1
eBook ISBN: 978-1-62747-195-4

Sojourn Publishing, LLC
280 Foothills South Drive
Sedona, AZ 86336

Dedication

This book is dedicated to you, the reader.
Whether you realize it or not,
you have come at this time in human history
as the seeds of the new being.
You have come to bring your gifts
and to share your wisdom.
Thank you.

Contents

Dedication...xi

Contents xii

Encoded Like a Seed... xv

Introduction..xvii

PART 1 The Foundation is Laid....................................1

   1 - New Year's Day 2007 3

   2 - Surprising Memories 9

   3 - Clearing the Air 15

   4 - Undercurrent's Message.......................................19

   5 - Giving Up on Normal 25

   6 - Miracles and Finding Jean 35

   7 - Mystery School 41

PART 2 The Journey...59

   8 - Veronica and the Communities 61

   9 - Setups and Stumbles 71

   10 - Messages from Colin's Toilet 77

   11 - Cliff Ahead – Preparing to Jump 81

   12 - On the Right Track 85

   13 - Going Beyond Forgiveness.................................89

   14 - Spirit of Tasmania 95

   15 - Date with Destiny...119

   16 - Moving Through Tassie....................................135

   17 - Tasman Peninsula 139

18 - Last Minute Assignments 145

19 - Freeing My Primal Self.................................... 151

20 - Seeding My Mind 161

21 - Storm Bay Assignment.................................... 169

22 - A Lifetime of Questions 179

23 - Asking for Help 183

24 - Isn't There a Nine Somewhere?........................ 185

25 - Flinders Island 189

26 - Wybalenna 193

27 - A Life Changing Meeting 197

28 - "We Gave You Wombats" 201

PART 3 The Aftermath................................**213**

29 - What Now? 215

Epilogue **227**

Afterword...**231**

Wholeness Alignment Process (WAP) **233**

Creation's Message – **The next book
includes a special gift for YOU!** **235**

Acknowledgements **237**

Contacts **240**

About the Author **241**

Feeling Inspired? What now?.............................**243**

Encoded Like a Seed

We all come into this world encoded like a seed . . . with our blueprint, what we are here for, what our gifts are, what we can become. Look at the oak tree, whose template is fully held inside the acorn. It is just waiting for the right conditions to express its full oak-tree self. We are the same. Within each one of us is a deep memory of our essence, what we're designed for, and what will fulfill us like nothing else.

The oak tree doesn't suffer self-doubt or criticize itself for being what it is. It doesn't compare itself to others and feel not good enough. Or wail that it doesn't know how to grow into a tree. It wears its oak leaves with certainty as it slowly grows into an enormous and beautiful tree, a full expression of its divine design.

Within every seed and within each one of us, is the urge, the whisper, that inclination . . . Showing us the direction, the path to the fulfillment of our destiny . . . Whether we recognize it or not.

Introduction

I was an accountant. Not an ordinary accountant, but that was my training. I tell you that to give you an idea of how my mind usually works. Logical, reasonable, based on facts. That's the world I'm comfortable in. And even though I've done some pretty outlandish things by most people's standards, I have always prided myself on having a firm grasp on reality. So, if you had told me in early 2007 that during a three-week period, my life would radically change — that I would quit my job, give away my beloved cat, and put my household in storage so I could travel halfway around the world — I would have chuckled, explained my financial situation and with certainty (the kind of certainty born in adherence to old patterns and ideas) denied the possibility.

And if you also suggested that the reason I was going to Tasmania was to connect with the spirits of the ancient Aborigines, I would have laughed out loud, and quickly muttered, "Fat chance of that happening!" with visions of pigs flying in my head. But I wouldn't have walked away until you brought up the whole "galactic portal" thing. That would have elicited a huge rolling of the eyes and a quick mental critique of your sanity before I evaluated how I could swiftly and safely exit the conversation. I was most definitely not a galactic kind of girl.

So you can imagine how hard it is for me to admit that the reality that unfolded before me was not logical or reasonable and in fact was way more challenging than I could have imagined. It was confusing, sometimes terrifying, yet always it brought a new sense of rightness: in the world, in God and Creation, and ultimately in myself. It brought me a deeper sense of my purpose for being on the planet.

From an early age, I always pondered the meaning of life, and especially the meaning of MY life. As an adult, I followed the "path" that was being modeled all around: career, marriage, financial success. Yet when I finally reached the peak of what was rumored to be the ideal life, I was disappointed and wondered, *Is this all there is? Is there really any meaning to life?*

At 33, after my initial awakening experience, I began my spiritual journey and searching for the truth, and I forgot about my life purpose. At that point I wasn't sure I had one. I felt like a rock, unconnected to guidance or knowing, and still feeling quite lost. I was surrounded by spiritual friends who had visions, heard messages, and experienced deep intuition, so I just figured I was either too dense or left-brained to be useful for much of anything in the way of purpose.

During the next twenty years or so, I started to read and hear about an enormous transition, a shift in consciousness that humanity was about to make. Every time this idea crossed my path, I would become fascinated, excited, passionate, intrigued. Somewhere deep within me I *knew* I was here to play a part in this happening – to help in some way I couldn't even fathom.

However, the idea I could help seemed absurd, so I just ignored it and thought I was crazy. Even though I was willing, I figured that kind of purpose was for other people, more gifted people.

During these same two decades, I gradually became deeply connected to Spirit. I also started to watch the signs, synchronicities, and patterns in my life. I began to see a way, however subtle, that I was being guided and led. My friends that could "see" would tell me things that validated the messages I was "getting" in my own subtle way. Perhaps I wasn't nuts; maybe I did have a part to play.

This is my story. This is how a logical, rational, people-pleasing, good-girl accountant finally, gradually, summoned up the courage to let herself be free. To jump off the cliff into becoming the person she was here to be. To emerge as someone who's willing to travel across the globe to meet a galactic portal she can't see and listen to beings she can't hear. To find the beginning of an unmarked path, *her* path, and follow, even though it was a total mystery and way outside her comfort zone.

I'm sharing my story, so you can see that even I, the rational rock, could learn to listen and follow the signs. I want you to see that I wasn't gifted, I wasn't special, and yet I was being guided along my path and assisted every step of the way — whether I recognized it or not.

Seems everyone these days is looking for their purpose: like we all suddenly realize we might have one. Do you fall in that category? Do you feel deeply that maybe, just maybe, you might have a gift to share or a part to play? Or is that idea so blasphemous or scary that you dare not think it?

We are all on this precipice of a monumental shift in consciousness, a quantum leap for all humanity. The Ancient Ones are calling us now, nudging us to find our way and do our part. We keep thinking it must be someone else's job, but I finally realized that I do have a part to play, and *so do you!*

We all have a life purpose, one that we chose for ourselves before we came into this lifetime. We've set up a roadmap to guide us, and helpers along the way so we don't get lost or stray too far.

Wherever you are on your roadmap, I share my story to encourage you to keep going. I share my "rock-ness," my confusion, my reliance on another's knowing, my subtle sense of rightness and moving forward without certainty. I share this to encourage you to embrace yourself and your path, however you may be experiencing it.

I was so self-critical because I didn't know my own gifts or even my own ways of knowing. What a waste of energy! I finally stumbled into my own "sense of rightness" in spite of tremendous self-doubt. I share my story to demonstrate that not everyone hears, knows, feels, or sees the same way. We are all different. We all have gifts. We all have ways we are guided within ourselves. You will have your own inner knowing, however it occurs for you.

I urge you, as you read, to pause and allow — even for a moment — your dreams to begin to rise up in you: to feel the niggle, the tickle, the softest brush of awareness dawning on you. Even go so far as to ask — to see, feel, or know, the calling of your future. Perhaps while you're reading about how I was guided through my journey, you'll pause and consider how guidance comes to you. Do you feel things in your gut, have thoughts you didn't think, maybe you hear a whisper or a voice, or get messages in your dreams? Wouldn't it be nice to be able to trust yourself and those deep inner feelings and to know you're not alone?

I share the unusual nature of my unfolding path to encourage you to embrace your gifts, your calling, and your uniquely beautiful self: even if it is different, challenging, and not what you expected. To give you strength to recognize your own soul-chosen, encoded life path as it unfolds before you. And lastly, to remind you to celebrate yourself.

We're all in this together. Thank you so much for being here in this wondrous time.

PART 1
The Foundation is Laid

Chapter 1

New Year's Day 2007

The first sound — I became aware of the birds singing.

How beautiful, I groggily whispered to myself.

"Ca ca ca ca ca ca." I became aware of Percy perched in the window watching the birdies with a different appreciation.

Wait! Why am I hearing the birds? An alarm went off within me. I was such a deep sleeper that I never hear the birds until after my clock screams at me a few times.

Why didn't the alarm ring? I wondered as I felt around the corner of the bed. I found the little clock and could tell the switch was off. Before I could panic further, I remembered …

It's New Year's Day, I don't need to get up. I thought with relief. Pulling up the covers, I curled on my side and started to drift off again until my bladder started to complain, bringing me back to consciousness.

Damn, I don't want to get up yet. Can you wait a little longer? I pleaded, but the bladder was insistent. Eyes still closed, I swung my legs out of bed to the floor. Without lifting my foot I pivoted, swinging my butt round to land perfectly on the toilet seat.

Hehehehehe, I laughed to myself. *There are definite advantages to living in such a small space!*

Still chuckling quietly, I finished and swung myself back around, hoping to slip back into bed without waking up entirely. Once again I snuggled under the comforter with my sleepy morning thoughts.

I wonder what kind of day it is. The thought prompted me to open one eye a tiny bit. I could see the sunlight filtering through the green leaves that filled the windows. That little squint caught the cat's attention and he was on me, purring.

"Good morning, Percy," I said in a sleepy voice, reaching out to pet him. "Happy New Year's." I grinned, "Do you have any resolutions you'd like to share?" I was amused at the idea. I hadn't bothered with resolutions for years. Seemed a waste of energy to think up ways to torment yourself for a day or two.

We snuggled for a while. He was probably the softest cat I'd ever owned, and it was always a great joy to pet him. But soon he wanted to go out. I reluctantly left my warm bed and shuffled a few steps to reach the door. The blast of cold winter air caused me to shiver: I turned the furnace up a bit and quickly curled up back in bed.

It was such a decadent and rare pleasure to just languish in my warm bed. Thoughtlessly, I listened to the birds and watched the leaves waving at me in the slight wind. Eventually I looked at the colorful stacks of clothes and bedding piled all around and above me. I was still amazed at how much stuff I had managed to fit inside my sweet little RV home.

I was even more grateful at how lucky I was to have it, after years of living with other people and never having my own space. *I still can't believe how generous Cathie and Ben were to lend me the money. I don't know how I would have made this transition otherwise.* It was a bit weird to wake up in an RV and put on a suit every morning to go be an accountant. *Good thing they don't consider your housing situation when you apply for jobs,* I chuckled.

I'm a bit disappointed though, with how things are going. I've been in Oregon three years now. It's been great to work again and remember that I'm competent and a hard worker and get along well with people. After nine years in the spiritual community, and three years of being sick, it has been great to discover I can live in the world and take care of myself. My thoughts rambled.

But I'm not very happy. Where's the sweetness in life? Where's the joy and the connection? It's New Year's Day, and I have absolutely nothing to do and no one to do it with. I've made some friends, but it feels like I'm not where I should be, AGAIN! I left Massachusetts because I kept feeling like I didn't belong there. Oregon had a definite sense of rightness, so here I am. I lay there thinking about the decision to move west, and the many connections and synchronicities that had encouraged me.

But when I came here I had two goals, to regain my health and to pay off my credit cards. That was the plan. And if I worked hard and kept at it, I would then be able to . . . I don't know what I thought happened then. A tear pooled in the corner of my eye.

Although I'm not as sick as I was when I was in New England, I haven't made much progress since I moved cross-country. I'm still tired and when I try to exercise it knocks me into depression. That's not right. And my digestion is still crap... literally! I laughed at my little joke.

And I haven't budged my credit card balances at all, in fact they've grown. Clothes for work, living expenses, blowing a head gasket on the way across country. I just can't seem to get ahead, I grumbled to myself, feeling discouraged.

Something's missing. Something's not right. This can't possibly be how I'm meant to spend my life. I feel like I'm on auto-pilot. I frowned at the thought and felt a grey cloud gathering overhead.

I lay there pondering my life and situation for a while, feeling more and more despondent. I knew I was on a slippery slope, but I was already past the point of caring. So it's a mystery to me how the next thought surfaced or where it emerged from. I suddenly became lucid.

"These goals aren't working!" I said out loud. "They are just not working, so I'm done with them." I could feel the finality and paused to see what was coming next.

"I need . . ." I stopped and scanned inside. *What do I need?*

"I need new goals," I stated without hesitation.

I waited and listened and then continued to scan my mind. *What do I want? What do I really want? More than health and clear credit cards; more than anything?*

As soon as I asked, I knew the answer. Was I brave enough to ask for it? Was I desperate enough to finally get out of my own way?

"I want to know what I'm here for," I whispered, feeling something shift.

"I want to find my path so I can fulfill whatever purpose I have for being here," I declared with growing certainty. This wasn't a new idea for me. But in that moment, something new was happening. My questions were flowing. *What do I need to do? What's in the way? What's blocking me from knowing my path or moving forward?*

As I pondered, I felt the answer begin to emerge from deep within me. I couldn't name it and I couldn't stop it, but I knew. I knew by the clarity, by the lucidity, I could feel something big about to be expressed.

"I give up. I surrender." I listened to what came out of my mouth with curiosity and wondered if it was true.

"I am ready and willing. It's time." I was surprised at the certainty with which this declaration was voiced.

At that moment, I could feel something peel away from me. Some sort of overlay was removed, and I felt open and vulnerable. I also felt full, calm, and serene. I could feel such a strong sense of rightness. I knew something had changed, and yet had no idea what it was. I laid there for a while and let this new "whatever" seep into my being.

I've had other moments, pregnant moments, when something changes me. Usually they are quite subtle and I never really know what they mean or what they are about. I assumed this was another one of those. So after a while I got up and went on about my day, expecting nothing to be any different in my world. Silly me.

Chapter 2

Surprising Memories

The rope is tight. My wrists are still raw from yesterday. I can feel the pain even before they pull the rope. I gotta stay conscious. Today I'll stay conscious. They don't like it when you pass out. It makes them mad and they get mean.

Waiting, waiting. Each moment of waiting is a moment of no pain. Yet each moment carries the dread of the pain to come. Each second is an eternity. I try to brace against the pull, but they wait. Sometimes they try to catch me off guard, but today they're just talking. Talking and laughing. It's all in a day's work to them.

I try to relax a little and still be ready. My heart is racing. So much adrenaline.

I won't make a sound today. They enjoy the screams. I hate hearing them laugh. But if I don't scream they'll just try harder. Oh my God! Dear God, please help me. Let them kill me today. Let me die into your blessed peace. Please help me.

I need to stay awake today. Yesterday they waited until I came to and started again. I can't do that today. I can't take another day of this. Oh please dear God let me die today.

Arrrrrrgggghhhh!   Arrrrrrgggghhhh!   Arrrrrrgggghhhh!
Arrrrrrgggghhhh! Arrrrrrgggghhhh! (Slump)

***

I found myself deep in the experience of the blight that I still carried from past incarnations of being bloodied and broken. I could feel the terror. I could feel the despair, the hopelessness. I had spent my entire life avoiding these memories: torture was what I feared most. Even as I child, exposed to movies, I wondered how we could be so brutal and cruel to another person.

"Sue?"

I jumped at the sound of the facilitator's voice. Dazed, I remembered I'm in a workshop, surrounded by women. They looked at me expectantly.

I gulped and began softly. "I'm grieving the intense cruelty that humans can perpetrate against other human beings. Torture is such a blight on the human soul. When you die and return to spirit, you don't notice it from that perspective. But as soon as you return in a body, you carry the effects with you. It's almost impossible to resolve it while you're here. And so it just leads to more cruelty." I moved to the edge of the circle and took a seat.

I'm sure the women were wondering what I was talking about, but they continued with their ritual and their own deep grieving and left me deep in thought.

Obviously the torture piece isn't finished for me yet. Please let this be healed in me, I whispered in my mind, then sat quietly and opened up. I scanned my mind and listened deeply, ignoring the guided meditation being facilitated in the room. However, one sentence cuts into my awareness: "And when you get to the bottom of the path, you'll find a door . . ."

The thought of a door, a way out of this recurring hell: it only took a moment, and I remembered the first time two years earlier . . .

I was going to the dentist to have my teeth scaled. No big deal. But sitting in the parking lot I went into abject terror for no reason. I had no specific memories, but I was bawling and hyperventilating. I have never been fond of dentists, but this was over the top.

Later that day, my housemate, Karen, did a regression with me to figure out what was going on. It was very intense as she gently guided me to go back and asked me to describe the scene. What could I see? What did I know? Usually I was wasn't able to see anything, but this time was different.

I could see the three men in black, on horses, that had come to my village and brutally killed everyone, women and children included. We were all hanging from the big old oak tree that we loved so dearly. Blood dripping everywhere. I was absolutely devastated that I could do nothing to save us. I felt traumatized by the memory.

Karen instructed me to go back in time .... To earlier, before the gruesome deed, and describe my surroundings.

We were a small agrarian village and deeply connected with nature. I was the head of the village, and we were a peaceful, happy bunch. I had a wife and children that I dearly loved: love such as I'd never felt in my current lifetime. I could see us around the hearth of our thatched-roof cottage. It was so simple and idyllic.

Then Karen asked me what I wanted to do.

Before I could have a single thought, my mouth opened: "We want to break the agreement with the other soul group. We hurt them and they hurt us. We keep taking turns, but we aren't going to go through with it. We BREAK the agreement."

Immediately I felt a release ripple out through consciousness like a pebble in a pond. I could feel how we were immediately freed, and so were they.

"Wow," said Karen, "your entire soul group is cheering and celebrating! I've never seen anything like it!"

We were both stunned by what had just happened. There was no thought in my answer, and I wouldn't have known it was even possible. But I felt so very different that it was obvious something had happened.

It was two weeks later when I returned to the same dentist that triggered this memory, and it was like a picnic on a spring day. At one point I even saw the three horsemen ride up to the stone fence and wave as they passed by.

By breaking the agreement that day, I had released my soul group and theirs from lifetimes of the karma we shared. And the trauma and memories were no longer in my body. I figured it was a one-off healing and never thought of it again except to remember the deep love I had experienced all those lifetimes ago.

Suddenly I'm back in the workshop, remembering this experience. Would it work here? I didn't wait for an answer . . .

I returned again to the feeling inside, the baggage that I've carried for millennia, *like a tear in the fabric of my being. Thank God I haven't had to play this one out in this lifetime,* I muttered silently. I know the soul often tries to find healing by calling to itself similar experiences on either side of the doing. Neither side escapes harm. The torturer is just as blighted as the tortured. You can't harm another without causing harm to yourself. And every lifetime, we are constantly trying to heal from these burdens we're not even aware of.

No wonder I've been afraid of torture my whole life, I thought before I dove into the process. I took a long, slow breath, and silently prayed for help. As I looked into my own heart, I found the knowing that we've been both the victim and perpetrator.

I would like to connect on a soul level with all the souls I've tortured or been tortured by in any lifetime. I couldn't feel them, but that was nothing new. I felt myself shift in awareness as connections were made on a deeper level.

I understand that we have made agreements to have these experiences prior to our incarnations, when we have no understanding of the horror or brutality to which we are agreeing. And even though the effects of these experiences leave us when we return to Spirit, whenever we return to a new body and life, they come with us like a curse on our soul. And try as we might to heal or release this in our lifetime, the depth of this wounding makes it almost impossible to do so: It's become embedded in our subconscious mind and cellular memory.

I let out a big sigh and hoped the others didn't finish too quickly because I knew I was onto something extremely important for me.

I've kept our agreements in every lifetime out of love and honor, but I've come to realize that it is not a loving act. It would be more loving to break these agreements. So I choose to break these agreements to torture, maim, brutalize, or terrorize, whether I was the perpetrator, or the victim. And as I free myself from these agreements, it frees you as well from the resulting effects or karma. My human mind balked at the audacity of this statement, but my soul remembered. I could already feel the bonds of cruelty starting to unravel in the human collective: it rippled out in waves and continued to expand. I felt the balm of something beyond forgiveness flooding my own heart as I remembered the truth.

I paused from my silent offering and noticed the swell of beautiful, happy energy now flowing through me. Not knowing if it was from my release or theirs, I continued.

I would like to disconnect from all the souls I have been connected with on a soul level. I felt the tension dissipate, and my body relax. *Beautiful.*

As the other participants started to stir, I sat there for a moment, becoming aware of the room and the talking. A bit more sharing and the workshop was over.

Something I hadn't even known I was carrying fell away that day. My logical mind was skeptical, not really believing in the possibility, or even the necessity. But the soul can hear and knows the truth. I walked out of the workshop with a lightness of step and sunshine in my heart. That was the third time I've dealt with those kinds of memories.

But it feels done now . . . I hope.

Chapter 3

Clearing the Air

I moved to a new RV park when I started to work in Salem. It was a big park, usually full, and surrounded on two sides by the highway. Its saving grace was that it was filled with towering old oak trees which buffered the roads, at least visually, and attracted squirrels and birds, which made the place feel more alive.

I had been living there for several months, when I went to Corvallis to see my healer friend, Nanci. After all the small talk and catching up, I decided to ask her advice.

"Nanci, the weirdest thing has been happening lately. I'm not usually a fearful person, but I keep having thoughts popping in my head of being attacked in some way," I explained as she was pouring a cup of tea. "I'm not sure why this is happening, but it is very unusual for me. I sometimes wonder if I'm having a premonition of some kind, but there's no real recurring theme. And these thoughts show up quite regularly."

"Hmmmm," she remarked, looking up from her tea. "Did you know that the prison is just a few miles from where you're parked?"

"No," I replied. "Why would that make a difference? When I walk around the park, I don't see shady characters or feel threatened in any way, except for these rogue ideas that pop in."

"Yeah, it does seem like a pretty nice place," she said, remembering her visits. "But when the prisoners get out, I'll bet many of them end up there because they don't have anywhere else to go. And besides, all those astral thoughts from all those inmates both in and out of prison would be hovering over the area."

"You really think that I'm picking up on their astral thoughts?" I queried skeptically, trying not to laugh.

"Well, not only their thoughts, but also all that astral debris that's accumulated there over the years." She sounded certain, so I decided to reserve judgment.

"Okay, maybe," I murmured, thinking about what I could do with this information. "Thanks, Nanci. I'll try a few things when I get home to see if I can at least clear the air over my parking spot." I chuckled a little as I said this, knowing I was unconvinced this "astral debris" was a real thing.

By this time in my life I was already quite used to other people being able to see and hear things I couldn't. So rather than pooh-pooh the idea, I decided it wouldn't hurt anything to give it a try. After all, it was all I had to go on, and I was tired of having my mind continually hijacked by these strange thoughts. They didn't feel natural to me, so maybe they weren't mine.

When I arrived home I could tell I was looking around the park differently, wondering if this neighbor or that were in fact recently out of prison.

I made sure to feed my favorite feral kitties first and especially that big old rough-looking guy I used to chase away. Boy, wasn't I surprised when my neighbor had him in her house and told me what a big old sweetheart he was. Definitely a great lesson in not judging a book by its cover.

I sat down at the table and pondered my conversation with Nanci, finally coming up with a plan. I closed my eyes, took a few deep breaths to calm down, and awkwardly began.

Holy Spirit and angels, if there are thoughts, energies or astral debris that don't belong to me: If these exist within my energy field, RV, or within my parking place, please clear them out now. I release them to go somewhere else, where they won't trouble me or anyone else.

I wonder if that worked, I mused quietly as I tried to feel a difference in the energy. I grimaced, realizing that I never really feel the energy, so why would I notice it now? I started to think about the inmates at the prison, and wondered whether they are bothered by the "astral debris" too. They would be swimming in it.

Hey, all you prisoners, are you suffocating in all that negative energy and astral debris? I found myself quietly addressing them all. *I have some angels here with some big vacuums. They're sucking it all up for me. If you want to get rid of what's troubling you over there, just toss it up here. They'll take care of yours, too.* I wasn't certain if this was true, but I loved the idea.

"And for you criminals that haven't been caught yet," I whispered, getting caught up in the joy of this possibility. "Toss yours up here, too. And all the victims of these criminals. They'll take yours as well. Everyone gets to jettison this crap today. It's a good day!"

I was smiling now and wondering again if this had done anything at all. It was fun, but I'd just have to wait and see.

It was several weeks later when Nanci stopped by the RV.

"Hey, Sue, how are you doing with your strange attack thoughts?" Nanci asked as soon as she walked in.

I was surprised at the question, and got quiet while I went looking for the answer. "Oh, my god, I hadn't even noticed! They're gone. I haven't had any. Not a one," I stammered, shocked at the realization. "I did some clearing. It must have worked."

Chapter 4

Undercurrent's Message

I loved the farmers' market. Lots of fun and friendly people, and lots of organic produce. Over time I had chosen my favorite farm stands, and tended to mostly buy from them. So it was noticeable to me one day when I bought some beets from a new Hispanic vendor. It wasn't that the beets looked better — they didn't.

Later that night while peeling the beets for dinner, something interesting started to happen. Another layer of thought was occurring to me. It was like receiving on two channels at once. Funny thing is, I wasn't hearing anything. But there was definitely another stream of thoughts running through my mind, in a sort of undercurrent.

I laid down the peeler and tried to listen in to see what was going on. I got a very clear sense of immigrants. I thought back to the Hispanic family at the market, but it was clear this flow of thought was not personal to them. I could feel immigrants and their struggles. And all that they endure, just trying to care for their families and find a better life. I could feel them suffering from being taken advantage of, disrespected, and even abused. I

19

could feel their silent torment, yet being unable to cry out for fear of being sent back.

I was puzzled about feeling these things. But it continued — to beyond here and now. I could feel how our country has been built on immigrants from the very beginning, and from all over the world. I continued peeling while I wondered why this was happening. Was it because I purchased the Hispanic family's beets? Was there something for me to know or do? Nothing came to mind but my normal little prayer . . .

"Holy Spirit, please bless the Hispanic family and all immigrants now working in this country with whatever miracles they most need," I whispered quietly while I put the beets in a pot. That felt good, and the undercurrent was now quiet.

I continued cooking in relative peace, except for Percy running like a mad cat up and down the RV. I was happy he'd discovered a way to let out some of his energy in a non-destructive way, knowing it could be so much worse.

"One of these days we're gonna figure out how to get you outside, Percy," I promised my gorgeous boy as I sat down to eat.

"Yum, I just love fresh beets!" I said aloud, looking at my beautiful plate. Percy had calmed down and was seated in the bench across from me watching me eat my meal. "I would give you something, you silly cat, but you never like my food. I think it's too healthy for you." I laughed and watched Percy to see if he would reply.

You're the silly one, waiting for your cat to respond, I thought with a grin.

As I sat quietly, I suddenly was aware of the undercurrent again. This time I was ready, and grabbed a nearby pencil and pad of paper.

It started with the prisoners, I heard quite clearly, without actually hearing anything aloud.

What do you mean? I silently queried.

More of them are ready now. I quickly thought back to my offer to the prisoners last month to help them clear the psychic debris they live with at the prison.

Okay, I thought slowly, *I suppose I can do it again. I hope I remember.*

The undercurrent was quiet, so I jumped in.

I'd like to connect with all the prisoners at the prison. I would like to offer you the opportunity once again to clear the psychic debris and negativity you have to live with every day — from your own mind, from the other inmates, and from all prior inmates. I'm requesting the appropriate angels to bring back their big vacuums and help us out. Just release what you don't want and they will take it to its next evolutionary level. I continued without a pause.

Then I could feel the undercurrent again — without words — and I got it.

I will leave this invitation outside of time and space. You can accept it whenever you want. If you're not ready now, no worries, it will be there when you are ready. All you need do is have a simple thought or wish — to be happier, to think more positive thoughts, to feel better about yourself. Whatever. I offered silently.

I began to wonder, *Can I really do it that way?*

Yes. The answer was clear and silent.

But does it take away their right to choose?

That's why it has to be an invitation. They all have free will to choose whether to accept your invitation or not.

Does it interfere with their own Soul's plan or with their karma? I silently asked whatever was communicating with me.

There are so many things that can be released at this time without the need to work out the karma. It used to be that during one's life you attempted to resolve these things. But it's become apparent that it is much more difficult to do that than anticipated, and humanity keeps digging itself in deeper and deeper.

We're in an unprecedented time of grace when much of that karma and even emotional baggage can be released easily. The problem is making humans aware of this.

I was writing as fast as I could, hoping not to miss anything. Fortunately, the undercurrent paused before continuing.

It's like an elephant that is chained as a baby. It becomes conditioned to being limited, so when it's an adult, it won't attempt to be free. It won't step outside the boundaries that it has grown up with.

Humans are like that. The key is how to get them to step outside the limitations of thoughts they accepted and discover that their old issues and karmic bonds are no longer there.

I was furiously jotting down notes, but my mind was also racing with thoughts and questions.

Is it possible to let ALL our issues go this simply? I blurted silently in the next pause.

No. There are some issues, beliefs, patterns of behavior and even situations which must be consciously recognized and worked through to resolution in each person's life. This is by their Soul's design and is to facilitate growth and experience. Their Soul knows what it can release and what it cannot. Another reason that all you can do is to invite, and then to leave it up to each soul to know how to respond.

As I finished my notes I realized I was sitting there alone in silence. I could no longer feel the undercurrent. And I no longer had questions. I stared at the pages in front of me and wondered how I could write something down when I couldn't hear anyone speaking. I read through the pages, and it was quite clear that there was information here that I didn't "know." These were not my thoughts at all.

I was a little unnerved by the experience. It was definitely a new one for me. I thought about this for a while, wondering if that was true or if I was going nuts. I remembered the incident in Albuquerque, which had been life-changing, but this was a whole new level of crazy.

Feeling somewhat uncomfortable with this new development, I sought distraction. I tucked the notes in my bookcase and promptly turned on the television. Time to while away another evening.

Chapter 5

Giving Up on Normal

For the first thirty-three years of my life, I was about as normal as I could muster. I tried to fit in, but it was pretty obvious to me that I didn't. I was always looking for my place, my people, somewhere I belonged. I marked each of my teen years with the latest identity I was trying on: volunteer, invisible, popular sorority girl, born-again Christian, hippie, nature enthusiast, and lover of parties.

Finally, at 19, I went off and joined the circus — we were all a bit different there. I started as a food vendor, worked my way up to "grace and beauty aloft on the single trapeze," fell on my butt and became office manager. Even there I kept morphing.

A few more years and I was married and wearing polyester pantsuits. We bought a house, both played rugby, and traveled to Europe. Before long I was getting my accounting degree, followed by becoming a workaholic. I had reached the American dream — accountant, married, house, car, money, and career. (Well, maybe no one dreams of becoming an accountant.)

But I had to face the truth — normal life didn't hold much interest for me. "There has to be more to life than this," was my constant lament. So I tried a few more things. After seven years of marriage, I was single again, still a workaholic accountant and traveling around the country for work.

I believed reality was what my eyes could see and there was nothing else to consider — until the episode in Albuquerque.

Incident in Albuquerque

I was working in Albuquerque for several months, so I rented a one-bedroom apartment and my friend Pam came to visit. It was a few nights into her visit when something happened — something life changing. The living-room and bedroom windows were open, just as they had been every night since we had arrived a week earlier. I usually don't leave windows open when I'm on the first floor, but Pam seemed quite comfortable with it. For some reason, though, this night it started to bother me.

It was just a passing thought at first — *Sue, close the window*.

No, you're just being silly, I told myself, getting ready for bed.

Sue, close the window.

Hmmm …. I decided to put the open ironing board in front of the window so if someone came in they would knock it over and wake me up. I continued getting ready for bed.

Close the window! CLOSE THE WINDOW!

Finally I got out of bed and shut the bedroom window with the thought, *Well, they won't be coming in here!*

As I was lying in the dark ready to fall asleep, it started again. It wasn't a voice, just a thought — a thought that I didn't really think. Yet I responded as if I had heard it.

Close the living room window.

But Pam likes having the window open, I thought, picturing Pam in her sleeping bag on the couch.

You need to close the window.

Pam's a big girl, she can decide for herself. I replied to that persistent thought.

Yeah, but could you live with yourself if she was raped? What if she was murdered? Are you willing to take that chance?

My "un-thought" thoughts had become quite insistent and to me quite insane. I figured I was just being paranoid, and wasn't willing to seem nuts to my friend. So finally I silently shouted — *SHUT UP!!!!!!* And then I fell asleep.

I'm an extremely heavy sleeper. I've had framed pictures fall off the wall and break two feet from my head and I couldn't wake up enough to see what the noise was, so what happened next was astonishing.

I woke up. I could hear muffled voices. In my grogginess, I just figured it was the people upstairs.

I heard it again. In my state of semi-consciousness, I remembered the word "nightmare" and thought maybe Pam was having one.

So, half asleep, I got up to wake Pam from her nightmare. I noticed the clock said 4:40. As I opened the bedroom door, I vaguely remembered I hadn't shut the door before going to bed, but I was too dazed to question it.

The apartment was barely illuminated by the light on the stove. I entered the dining room and looked into the living room, seeing my worst nightmare. A dark shadow was crouched over Pam on the couch. He had heard me come in and he quietly said, "Don't scream or I'll hurt your friend."

Without a thought I latched onto his suggestion and let out a scream that came from the depths of my being. It was LOUD, and it was long. I had no idea I could scream like that! Pure instinct, and a gut sense of "no frigging way!" He was out the window before I was finished.

***

Obviously that was a terrifying experience, and it took both of us a while to recover. But while I was processing the experience, running it through my mind over and over, I began to recognize something incredible.

I realized there was something watching out for me and helping me. Something that had the ability to get into my thoughts to warn me and use the words in my head to guide me into action. And "it", or should I say "they" — they even woke me, the heaviest sleeper on the planet, in the middle of the night, when all I could hear were muffled voices.

Ever since that night, I've listened to what shows up in my mind, knowing it's not always just my little thoughts or paranoia. Rather than just thinking I was nuts, I began observing and considering these random thoughts. And I've started watching for how thoughts feel — do they spring from my thinking, or do they pop up in a seeming unrelated way?

Almost overnight, I began trusting "them." I just figured it was a guardian angel or some such thing, and I was grateful for the help. I felt deeply that if I listened, I'd be guided and directed in ways that would surprise me. The more I listened, the more wonderful things began happening for me. As amazing things happened, the more I thanked these unknown helpers. The more I thanked them, the more they seemed to help.

I had moved through life pretty much like most people, not thinking about where hunches and whims come from, just making decisions based on normal thoughts. Yet this experience in Albuquerque gave me such a strong feeling of not being alone. That could have made me uncomfortable, but instead I felt lucky or blessed or protected in some way.

***

Shortly after my awakening, in 1986, I quit normal life and filled the years with wanderings and adventures — unconsciously testing the limits of grace. This included lots of world travel, nine years in a spiritual community studying A Course in Miracles, and three years of being sick, depressed, and suicidal.

When I finally emerged from that Dark Night of the Soul, I was whole, I was clear, I was ready to move forward with my life's purpose. If only I knew what it was.

I was hoping to find a path with a big road sign that says "SUE, THIS WAY" so I couldn't miss it and would know for certain that it was mine. But what I found instead were crumbs and clues and pieces of the puzzle. Sometimes I could feel they were important when I stumbled upon them, but without a big picture, I couldn't see how they would ever fit together. So I collected these in my being and carried them, without even knowing it.

I considered myself to be as intuitive as a rock, which is not to knock rocks in any way — but I felt that dense. I was smart, but even after my awakening, I didn't see things or hear things like all my psychic and clairvoyant friends. I didn't even have the same awareness or knowing as my intuitive friends.

I found this quite frustrating for the longest time, and was constantly looking for what was blocking me. What did I need to do to open up this gift? It didn't help that all these psychics would take one look at me and assume I could already see.

It took decades for me to get comfortable with myself, and stop comparing myself to others. I knew I was being helped; that was obvious from my life. And somewhere along the way it occurred to me that maybe, just maybe, I was different for a reason — designed for a different purpose.

Eventually I heard the word "claircognizant" — someone who just knows. Time stood still for a moment and I immediately recognized: that was me — that was my gift. Did that mean I suddenly trusted myself or knew what to do? — I wish.

It took decades of trial and error, self-doubt, and feeling deeply into my heart, gut and mind. I learned how to watch for signs and follow inklings and clues and whispers to my soul. The more I trusted myself and the beings that helped me, the more my life flowed and I lived in *grace*. As I acknowledged the help I was being given, they seemed to be even more audacious in their help. To these I am forever grateful for their patience as I stumbled along this path.

Surfacing again in the world after all that wandering and illness was an interesting adventure. I still didn't feel like I fit in, but I had a deep, deep foundation of connection now, with the Divine and with myself. I was again the luckiest person I knew, but it was different now. I knew EVERYONE had the capability to be lucky, to be blessed, to access miracles.

After moving to Oregon, I worked hard, made friends and settled into a more normal life. And frankly, "normal life" wasn't any more satisfying than the first time. I looked for meaning, and useful things to do.

It had been two decades earlier when I had such an intense knowing that I was on the planet to do something to help humanity through a magnificent evolutionary leap in consciousness. I *knew* it. Anytime this quantum leap was mentioned, I was riveted, excited and more than ready to do it. If only I knew what I was going to be doing.

I studied things to help with my health, and was inspired to offer what I learned to others. I was sure the Depression Resource Center was going to be my way of helping. I had been through the depths and had found my way out. Surely I would be fantastic at helping others balance their brain chemistry and hormones and health.

I started to set it up, but couldn't seem to get it happening. I worked with friends and family on the phone with great results. But you can tell very clearly when there is no flow to your plan, it feels like trying to push a rope uphill.

The Whisper or the 2x4

I'd noticed over the years that there are often "set ups" to entice us down our path, and also brick walls preventing us from getting sidetracked or distracted. It's not that we don't have choices, we did choose — before birth — and we made deals with our guides and the Universe to keep us on track.

When it's time to make a change or take action, the guidance starts sending us messages. Initially the messages are gentle. There will be little whispers, "turn here," "go talk to that person," or "take that course." Or maybe you suddenly find yourself pondering something new — going to Canada, painting, becoming a naturopath, or writing a book?

And if you've brushed these messages aside, which many of us do, have you noticed they get more direct or insistent? You head the opposite direction, and suddenly you find yourself right back in the same situation. You avoid something, and then everyone you meet is telling you the magic message, even the TV. The universe is conspiring to get you to where you want to be in spite of yourself.

Have you ever totally ignored the nudging, the signs, the urgings, and finally the yelling, until you've been forced down the path? I call this the 2x4. Often this is illness or accident, catastrophe or chaos, until we've learned the lesson, made the move, changed our life. It is challenging and we learn lots, but it isn't fun. It pries from our fingers the lifestyle, lover, or beliefs we cling to as if our life depends on it. Ultimately, we discover our greater *Life does* depends on letting go and either going with the flow or moving in a new direction.

I preferred to go with the whisper, especially after being hit with the 2x4 a time or two. I was always watching, waiting, looking for a sign, the path, and the way to go, so I could find my way — preferably with ease and grace. I just needed a clue which direction it was. Like the Fool in the tarot deck, I was willing to go anywhere, do anything, follow any path, whatever I was called to — just give me some clarity!

I already KNEW that if I did what I was called to do, life would be wonderful, graceful, satisfying, and fulfilling — even if not always easy. I also KNEW if I resisted, avoided, or tried not to go where I was meant to go, that life would be awful — feeling wrong, out of sorts, and not be much fun.

I was always watching for the wave. In surfing, if you catch the wave, there's lift, there's energy, there's flow, and there's movement. If you miss the wave, you're dead in the water. You don't have much choice but to paddle hard or to wait for the next wave.

When you miss a wave, when you miss your Plan A, the Universe will come up with a Plan B for sure, but this takes time — sometimes lots of time.

I've had to wait a few times for Plan B to cycle through, or Plan C, D or K. Not a fun way to spend time. Feeling out of the flow. Feeling lost. Feeling like you're in the wrong place.

This "whisper or 2x4" is happening to all of us now as we experience this quickening of time and feel the impetus to move into alignment with our Divine Self and our soul's purpose. You're not nuts, you're not alone, and there is more help available to you than you realize, to move through these times with ease and grace.

When I read the Tao of Pooh, I was so inspired by Winnie and his Woo Way Day. So much so, that I aspired to have a Woo Way Day every day – to just wander through, following the signs and clues, and see where you end up.

But after my illness and move to Oregon, I felt stuck again — lost. Like I was following a path that had suddenly emerged from the woods into a clearing. And standing in that clearing, I couldn't see which direction the path went or what was next.

So when I woke up on New Year's Day 2007 and changed my goals, everything changed. I had accidentally aligned with my purpose — with my Divine intention. Within days the wave came and picked me up. And this time I wasn't going to miss it, no matter what.

Chapter 6

Miracles and Finding Jean

Three days after my "big surrender" I found the first "crumb" to help me find my way, although it was unrecognizable at the time. It was an email invitation to a Miracles Mastery Symposium in Portland.

I had heard of two of the speakers, and knew them both to be dynamic and inspiring, but neither were enough to make me interested in straining my credit cards further. Yet I had a vague sense of needing to go, having no idea the impact it would have.

I signed up, and two weeks later I was there with friends. As I wandered through all the tables of products and information, one postcard caught my eye. It was advertising Jean Houston's Mystery School. I had never heard of Jean Houston, and I didn't know what a mystery school was.

Probably another person who's learned a few things trying to sell it as more than it is. Boy, was I ever wrong on that one.

When they finally introduced the evening presenters, I recognized the name of the Mystery School lady. Apparently Jean Houston was a well-known pioneer in the human potential movement. She shared the program with Peggy Rubin, her long

35

time co-presenter. I was curious what they would be sharing, and within minutes my mind was reeling!

Oh my God! How did I never know this woman existed? Was the first thought that blurted through me.

She's the closest thing to my people I've ever heard, was the next spontaneous thought, one that I wouldn't understand until later.

If I hadn't been afraid and stifled myself, I would be like her. This last thought seemed absolutely blasphemous, but whatever was surfacing within me was not pausing for censorship, instead racing into my consciousness while I was distracted by the program.

I was riveted. Jean's thought process was so refreshing and so enlivening that I felt like I was being ignited by her words. I could barely sit still I was so stirred up. Peggy was masterful in her own right and brought the presentation to life with her theatrical energy. The program was both inspiring and entertaining and went places that were entirely new to me. But it was Jean's thought-provoking questions that took me to unfamiliar depths. I was captivated.

It was almost over when she asked the question that released a virus into my being. "What idea or impulse has been circling your head like a swarm of flies pestering you for your whole life? What is your essence? What is your lineage?"

That idea, that I was something I hadn't yet discovered, but that was already working and growing in me – that idea was mesmerizing. Like the acorn that is destined to become an oak, something within me already knew what I was and where I was going.

I could feel the virus moving through my being, triggering unknown connections, unlocking hidden secrets, releasing the contents of Pandora's Box. I was swirling inside with possibility and knowing, as my conscious mind looked desperately for a thought that would make it feel safe or normal again.

After the program, I picked up the postcard about Jean's Mystery School and headed to my room, knowing deep within me that I needed to work with this woman.

I woke the next morning, still on fire, with the fever of that virus running rampant within me. By lunch I remembered that I'm an alchemist. Not really grokking the full import of that revelation, I was absolutely certain that was my lineage, my essence, and what I was born to express in this life.

The program continued with other speakers, and I was as attentive as I could be, but inside was a steady stream of consciousness flowing, unleashed by Jean's idea of being all you can be and expressing your full potential.

My friends were patient with me. An unknown woman who joined us for lunch felt compelled to tell me that she was intuitively seeing me writing books that would help lots of women. Another woman felt called to give me $500 to help me go to Jean's Mystery School.

I was daunted only slightly when I discovered the price of the Mystery School program, but with the $500, a 20% discount and the ability to pay monthly by credit cards, nothing was going to stop me. I KNEW this was the direction to go – this was the path to my future.

Even as I drove home on Sunday afternoon, my mind was still racing about what was possible. I was flooded with ideas of programs that would help humans release the subconscious baggage they were carrying but no longer needed.

I remembered what "they" had told me recently, about the prisoners. That if I could get humans to step outside the confines of their mind and what they feel binds them, they would realize they were free.

I kept hearing repeatedly — in my non hearing way — *give me 100 Viet Nam vets and some EMDR practitioners and we will be able to quickly and easily deal with their PTSD.*

We've all heard the hundredth monkey study, where researchers discovered that if a new behavior was adopted by 100 monkeys, that suddenly, without direct exposure, monkeys all over neighboring islands would be adopting the same behavior.

In my own life, I could think of two instances where I had been seeding the human collective unconscious with new thought patterns without knowing it.

I thought back to my divorce, which was so amicable that our joint lawyer charged us less than the minimum.

And when I was scheduled for a hysterectomy to remove a large mass, my mom kept saying, "it's going to be painful" and "you could have cancer." I refused to join her in those beliefs. Later I would realize that I was leaving a new pattern of thought within the collective as another option. Rather than the usual — being afraid, terrified, and expecting the worst — I knew I was moving in grace. When it was all over and my parents were flying home, my dad's words said it all: "This was more fun than misery — for everyone."

I already knew it was possible to change the world by changing the human collective — to seed it with new ways of dealing with old situations.

I knew I would need funding. I brainstormed what I would do with $1 million if I won the lottery. I also decided that if I had $100,000 to start with, I could easily produce the materials needed to fund-raise for this important cause.

At the time, I wouldn't have been the least bit surprised if someone suddenly handed me the $100,000 to begin these programs. I was actually quite surprised when it didn't happen. This would have been discouraging, except the first Mystery School weekend was coming up. Who knew what would show up then?

***

My experience at the Miracles weekend may have been the first time I recognized it, but it was the beginning of receiving downloads of ideas, information, and knowing. Initially, my rational mind tried to sort it all out and make a plan. That didn't work.

Eventually I realized that while the insights were flowing, I needed to just let them flow. I began to welcome these snippets of awareness with open arms, not judging them, but just receiving them as best I could. They were pieces to my puzzle — the crumbs on my path guiding me. I learned to collect them up, tuck them someplace safe and carry on, trusting that time and guidance would eventually make sense of it all.

Chapter 7

Mystery School

My destiny had been calling me for more than a decade now. It started around the time I heard of Barbara Marx Hubbard and her book *The Revelation: A Message of Hope for the New Millennium*. It wasn't the book that caught my attention, but a story from it that someone shared with me. About how, in the next 20 years, humanity would progress exponentially. In that short period, we would change as much as we had from being cavemen until now.

That idea so caught my interest and curiosity — I was riveted by the question it stirred in me. How would you enable that enormous of a change to occur in the least disruptive way possible? I could imagine a caveman suddenly showing up in today's world. He wouldn't recognize anything. Not the landscape with its roads and buildings, not the vehicles, not the people with our glasses and dyed, styled hair, jewelry and clothes. Not even the domesticated animals and hybridized plants. It would all look so foreign and would feel even stranger with all the noise, the EMF radiation, and music.

So I pondered this question in meditation and could see that you would use stories to expand the mind — to stretch the mind enough for new possibilities to enter. When the story was finished, the mind would snap back, but it could never return fully to its previous tightness. So you would continue with more and more mind-opening stories.

This made me think about the TV shows — *Star Trek* being one of the first I remember. And the movies and books: *Powder, Groundhog Day, The Matrix,* and so many more. I could see that somehow there was a crack in reality, and these far-fetched and amazing stories were trickling down into the minds of authors, writers, and directors, allowing the new ideas to germinate — first in their minds, then in ours.

Star Trek the Next Generation alone was responsible for some serious stretching of my mind around consciousness and what it is and if it is actually tied to the body.

It was during all of this deep pondering that I began to recognize my reaction to the idea of a quantum leap for humanity. Where exactly it was seeded I don't remember, but it invoked in me such deep feelings of certainty and rightness. I began to realize it was for this leap that I was here. That somehow in a way I could not yet fathom, I was here to help humanity through this transition with grace.

So when I landed in the Mystery School I was in heaven. Here were amazing people talking about reaching their full potential, and Jean was the great way-shower in this regard. Her work basically legitimized what had been happening to me, gave me words to describe what was going on, and concepts to help me understand. It also catalyzed forward movement on my path.

The program was set up as eight weekends and a full week during the summer. The program was in its 24th year and many of the 100 women and a handful of men had been coming for years.

Each weekend was amazing in its breadth, and would include ritual, dance, theatre, meditation, and lectures by Jean. There were always some interesting or inventive processes offered that would enable you to access more of the Divine being you carry – and empower you to express this in your daily life. And even though I was unaware of being changed, I am certain that I was upgraded into more of my full potential without realizing it until much later.

Every meal I sat with a new group, and it was quickly apparent this program had been life-changing for most of them. I was constantly amazed and impressed with the participants — and encouraged as well. This group was clearly not closed-minded or in any way inhibited from expressing their brilliance in the world. Many knew their purpose, and were busy making a difference to someone somewhere.

On Life Purpose

It was during these weekends that my thoughts about life purpose clarified. I could see, looking at these people, that missions come in all shapes and sizes. Like a field of wildflowers, we're all different, yet designed perfectly for our individual destiny. Some people are here to change the world, others are here to have an amazing and beautiful loving relationship, or to raise a family. Some are here to bring in new technology, or invent something that solves a major issue with the earth. Others are meant to have money and comfort and live a life where they take good care of themselves.

No matter what it is, your calling is *your* calling, your unique gift to share with the world — creator of beauty, nurturer, artist, musician, philosopher, parent, scientist, inventor, investor, leader, raising the new kids, implementer of new ideas that change the world in large or small ways. We all have one — a mission, destiny, life purpose, soul calling, or passion.

It took me an embarrassingly long time to realize that comparing myself to someone else was a great way to self-sabotage. But judging or criticizing myself for the path that was calling me was even worse. I would go through periods trying to fit in and not be so "out there." When I didn't listen to my inner guidance, I was miserable, depressed, and everything would go wrong. I would be moving through my life as if on auto-pilot and often I would get sick – again.

When I decided to go with my gut no matter how "unusual" it seemed to the world – or to me – I was not only happy, but everything would fall into place magically. This recognition certainly made choosing a whole lot easier.

The Gifting

I was fifty-four at the time, and was on the younger edge of the spectrum in Mystery School. Nowhere else had I ever encountered such vibrant and alive women in their '60s, '70s, '80s and beyond. It made me realize that growing older doesn't have to embody the gradual decline that is the status quo. These women and men were beyond inspiring, and stirred in me the desire to live my fullest life possible and to fulfil my destiny.

It was the May weekend that particularly stands out in my mind — the Gifting. Everyone offers their gifts freely to others. I was too shy and uncertain of myself to offer anything, but I was a happy participant and was repeatedly blessed by the gifts of others.

The highlight of the weekend was the gift Jean offered. They created a sort of flowing and colorful tent in a quiet room. Jean entered into an altered state and waited for each person to enter and ask for something they wanted. This went late into the night as 100 people individually entered Jean's tent for this blessing. There were rumors of babies born and love found over the years of this tradition, so I was very excited.

It was a deep, intimate time where you asked for what your heart desired — that which you really wanted. I had thought deeply about this while I was driving there. It wasn't a hard decision, and I just went with what came to mind — fertile ground.

I wasn't positive what that meant, but I could feel it. I needed fertile ground to grow. To blossom and bloom into my full potential. I knew there was something amazing growing in me, and I needed fertile ground to help it to thrive and flourish. I wanted to let it blossom into its fullness, even though it was still a seedling within me.

When my turn came and I entered, it all felt very normal. Not as mystical as I expected. Jean asked me what I wanted, and I stated my request. She asked me a few questions, and then asked me if I was coming to the Social Artistry program later in the summer.

I told her no, that I couldn't afford it. I was barely affording the Mystery School.

She said it was important for me to come, and told me to go talk to Julia, the office manager. I should tell her that I would be an assistant for that program and coming at cost. And then we were finished.

I had no idea at the time if she had worked her magic or not. And I was unfamiliar with the Social Artistry program. But even so, I was delighted to be invited and knew it would be a remarkable opportunity.

This meant going to the Mystery School week, a week back at work, followed by the Social Artistry week. It wasn't long before I got a strong, distinct knowing – one I've only had a few times in life. This three-week period in July, 2007 was going to be life-changing.

I was definitely excited and also curious — what sort of change was coming? If you had told me then — where this would take me — I never would have believed it.

Three Weeks That Changed Everything

I entered into the Mystery School week with great anticipation, and joined in fully. Jean and Peggy were on fire, sharing so many inspiring talks and amazing experiences. The participants were definitely a highlight, and it was great to reconnect in a deeper way with many of the regulars as well as meet so many wonderful new people. But the woman who caught my eye from the beginning was Margot from Australia. I made a point of finding time to connect with her. She had established a successful company in Australia that helps managers and CEOs clear out their emotional baggage so they can be exceptional at their jobs. I was fascinated by her stories, and could definitely see parallels between her work and mine.

We became friends, and had many intense and passionate discussions about fulfilling a life's purpose. As we talked about finding ways to move forward with it, I told her about my shift on New Year's day. Gradually I opened up and told her about the episode of breaking the agreement to be tortured and having the effects so totally leave my life. She was intrigued, to be sure.

She looked at me deeply and said, "We need to do a regression with you but into the future so you can see what's coming ... What you're here for."

I practically jumped in her lap, I was so excited. "Yes, please! That sounds amazing!" I *knew* this was an important thing to do.

The week was really busy, and it was the last night at a fairly casual dinner to celebrate. Lots was going on, everyone caught up in their own conversations. I don't know who sought out whom, but it was definitely obvious — *now* is the time.

We sat quietly on the couch in the middle of all the comings and goings. She put me into a hypnotic state, which felt different from the regressions I'd experienced. I was conscious and aware, but I also knew if I wanted to open my eyes or get up that I wouldn't be able to.

She instructed me to move forward along my timeline, first two years out . . . Nothing, then one year out . . . Nothing. When we got to six months, I was still seeing nothing.

How strange, I thought. *I wonder if I'm leaving the earth.*

Before I could ponder further, she returned me to the room. I looked at her a bit dazed with a quizzical look on my face.

"There's something missing," she offered quietly. "I couldn't see anything, not even in six months. It's obvious to me there is something that is missing."

"I wonder if I die or something." I said, hoping she'd hear it as a question.

"No, that doesn't feel like it," she said thoughtfully. "It's like there's a piece to your puzzle that you haven't yet found. And until you do, the future isn't available to be known. I wonder if you have some sort of decision or choice to make."

"I don't know," I replied in a dazed way. "I guess I have some questions to ask Spirit. And some people to talk to. But thanks so very much for doing that."

As I drove home to work for a week, I deeply pondered this question about what was missing. I had such a deep sense that I am on the earth for a purpose, but felt so lost in how to find my way or move forward.

I called Hart on the way home and set up a session for the next morning.

The Missing Piece

I had started seeing Hart six years earlier when I was having major health issues. After getting some bad water in Hong Kong, my body was full of parasites, bacteria, and viruses — so many nasties it seemed to be shutting down. It took me a while to discover her, but once I did, I was finally getting some real help.

She had trained in biology, and had extensive knowledge of herbs, homeopathy, and essential oils. But the most amazing thing about Hart was her ability to muscle test without touching a body. She would just feel it in her own body. And her accuracy was nothing short of phenomenal.

Remember: I'm an accountant. I can't help but audit everything that's said and done around me — at least it used to be that way. But she would pick up on things that seemed impossible for her to know, yet I knew they were true.

She would have me sniff an essential oil, and she'd watch the energy move through my system and see where help was needed. Then she would start asking quietly — on which level was the issue: physical, emotional, mental, and spiritual. And if it was emotional, she'd ask if it was childhood, past-life, what age, was it a belief, was it something you were taught. So many possibilities, but she would move quickly through them until she zeroed in on something. And then she'd address it in the most surprising and effective ways.

At the end of each session, I would feel certain that I had received the best possible help to heal not only my body, but all of me. I believe she saved my life, or at least saved me from a life of illness.

As I crawled out from under the health issues, and later the depression — my Dark Night of the Soul — I felt quite lost, with no idea how to re-enter life. That's when Hart's amazing ability to test and diagnose underlying causes became essential to me. Looking back decades later, if I hadn't known Hart, I don't think I would ever have become confident enough to do what I'm here to do. She's the one I called when unusual things began to happen to me. I would tell her my strange inklings and experiences and then quite seriously ask if I was nuts. Of all the people I've known, her integrity is impeccable, and I trust her completely.

One of my favorite things about how Hart works is when she ranks things on a scale of one to ten — one being harmful, ten being stellar. It made things so clear to my accountant mind — you can't argue with numbers. So when I was trying to make choices I would often ask her to test them in this way. An eight was transformational, and rarely would anything test higher, but I would occasionally get a nine.

I have been given quite a lot of flak over the years because at critical times in my decision making, I have consulted Hart. So many people believe you need to do it on your own and not ask for help. I understand, but I believe if the Universe sends you help, then receive it fully. We all know the story of the person on the roof praying to God to save them from the flood, and then turning down two boats and a helicopter. I was sent remarkable help in Hart. There's no way I wasn't accepting it.

She was like training wheels for me, and that was such a blessing. Initially, so much of what she told me validated what I had already felt or known, but was too uncertain to trust. This strengthened me enough that I started to timidly share with her what I "thought" I knew. Well, I wasn't always right, but I wasn't always wrong either.

I started watching and feeling and seeing what was validated and what wasn't. I discovered that I didn't just blindly follow, but would know when I needed to follow my own knowing and not her suggestion.

Not everyone offering intuitive, psychic, or clairvoyant information does so with integrity. Early on I would constantly state my intention for the highest and the best, and to fully align with my Divine Self. And my gut feeling, however subtle, steered me away from many "seers" with less than the highest integrity or ability.

The first day I went to Hart for my health, I knew she could help me — I *knew* it. I thought it was just about the physical, but she turned out to be an essential piece in my finding my path and my purpose and I will be forever grateful.

***

I was hurrying around the RV trying to get ready for work. This was difficult to do while holding the phone to my ear.

"So Sue, how can I help you?" Hart asked in her direct, matter-of-fact way.

"I just got back from Mystery School, which was great, but I had a really interesting experience there," I paused collecting my thoughts.

"Okay, tell me."

I proceeded to fill her in on my regression with Margot and how it had left me with a big question and no answers.

"Hart, my question is this — can you see that something is missing?"

"Yes," she responded quickly, and I know she's already testing.

"Is it a person, a place, a thing, an idea, or what?"

"It's a location, Sue."

"Australia!" I chirped, enthusiastically.

Hart paused and slowly faltered over her answer, "Nooooooooooooooooo."

Undaunted, I kept going, "Europe?"

"No."

"Asia?"

"No."

"South America?"

"No."

"Africa?"

"No."

"Russia? Antarctica? Iceland?"

"No, no, no," Hart laughed.

"Well, where else is there?" I asked in frustration.

"Sue, why was Australia such a wobbly no?"

I paused with her question, and suddenly *knew* the answer.

"It's Tasmania," I suggested quietly and with certainty.

"You're right Sue, it's Tasmania. How did you know that?"

"I don't know, I just suddenly *knew*. As soon as I had the thought, I knew it was right," I marveled, and was once again grateful for Hart's validation of one of my "unthought" thoughts.

We both sat there quietly for a moment, letting the magnitude of that realization sink in.

"Sue, the piece that needs to drop in is not in this world," she mentioned slowly. "It's having access to a greater part of you. You'll need to go to Tasmania and have the indigenous people show you to the location where this gets activated in you."

"So what's this look like? A two-week visit or what?" I was already worrying about the finances.

"Sue, I think you're going to need to go for five months."

I had heard the words, but I needed to stop to let them sink in. "Five months? I can't afford to go for five months," I said softly. My mind was spinning at the thought. "I don't even know that I can go at all."

"Well, Sue, think about it and see what you can do." There was no judgment in her words.

I glanced at the clock and realized I was going to be late.

"Hart, I gotta go to work." Awkwardly, I slipped on my suit jacket. "What would I do for five months?" I asked as I checked my hair in the mirror.

"I don't know, Sue. I think it's one of those things that will just unfold as you go. You know how to do that. You've done it before."

I chuckled nervously at that comment knowing how true it was. I grabbed my briefcase, gave my kitty a quick cuddle, and headed out the door, still carrying the phone.

"Oh, I don't know, Hart. I wish we could talk longer, but I gotta go to work." As I climbed into the car, I had a sudden moment of clarity.

"Hart, if I don't go to Tasmania, will I still be able to fulfill my destiny — to do what I'm here to do on the planet?" I was shaking inside. I knew that this was *the* deciding question. I could feel time slowing down, and I held my breath half afraid to hear the answer.

"No."

So simply put, yet my whole world shook. Half elated, half despairing, I started the car.

"All right, I'll keep you posted. Thanks so much for your time."

Stunned, I sat in the car for a moment and looked around the empty campground. My little RV looked so cozy nestled in the trees. So many trees and barely any people, it was such a peaceful place. After two years I had finally found a place to park my RV where I felt comfortable and safe. I had settled in. With a heavy sigh, I drove away.

My thoughts were racing as I headed to work. After years of being dead in the water, I had finally found the trail again. I couldn't not go. I couldn't risk more years of treading water and wondering where I had gone wrong. Or waiting for Plan B to circle round again.

I was free to choose, I knew that. But I could feel it rising up in me. That familiar feeling. That feeling you get as you head for the cliff and know you're about to jump. Even though part of you wants to stay put, the momentum to jump carries you along.

Surprising Encouragement

I let my call with Hart sink in slowly as I went sleepwalking through my next week of work. I couldn't wait to head back down to Ashland for the Social Artistry Program. So much was swirling within me, and I couldn't think of a better place to be.

You'd think a week of accounting would have allowed my rational mind to get sensible and talk me out of making any rash decisions. But my logical mind had learned years ago that it was just a facade for the heart and the gut who really make the decisions. In recent years, my dedication to follow the true calling of my soul definitely shifted the rational mind's functioning in this team. So the left brain did what it knew to do to support the whole; it looked for the options, the possibilities, and the worst case. The long drive gave me lots of time to think.

Rather than tell myself all the reasons why I couldn't do this, I decided to try on the decision — imagine I was doing it. What would it look like or feel like? How could I go and still pay my credit-card minimums? How much vacation did I have coming?

"What's the worst-case scenario?" I laughed out as I spoke. My mind loved playing this game.

"You jump off this cliff and end up months later penniless, without a job, and not knowing what to do next." I paused at the sobering scenario.

"Well, that's where you were two years ago when you landed in Oregon," I snickered. "You didn't starve. You got work after not having a normal job for eighteen years. You made friends and it turned out fine. It'll never be that hard again."

Promises, promises, something inside me quipped.

I arrived in Ashland soon enough, causing the inner chatter to pipe down. I was a volunteer for the week, helping Julia, Jean's wonderful Office Manager, with whatever she needed. It was easy work and quite fun and we got on really well. I was still able to participate fully in the program, which was fantastic.

There were some amazing and inspiring speakers there. Jean and Peggy were fantastic as always, and it was in one of Jean's meditations when it started to happen. She had directed us to actively meditate in a very kinesthetic way. We were up and moving around, yet inwardly aware of being someplace else. I was deeply surprised to find myself working with indigenous people to apologize and ask for forgiveness for my ancestors. This was more intuition than I was known for, so I just figured it was a fluke and went with it.

At the break I went to the bathroom, and while sitting on the toilet, eyes closed, a black face appeared before me. It was decidedly an Aboriginal face although I couldn't tell the gender. I could see its lips moving, but couldn't hear what it was saying. An unusual experience for me.

Later, when I was reconnecting with the regular Mystery School attendees, I would casually mention that I was thinking about going to Tasmania. People's reactions startled me.

"Oh my goodness, my hair is standing up all over!" said several, showing me their arms.

"I have chills, Sue, that's a great sign that you're meant to go," offered others with either chills or truth bumps.

The responses were varied and some would give me messages they were intuiting that were positive and excited.

It was the Native American woman who made the pine needle turtles – her message went the deepest and said the most. She got that far-away look one has when receiving messages and said, "You are going to Tasmania. You've been called and they are waiting for you. You will do great work there. Sue, my whole body is vibrating." I stood there stunned, as I could *feel* throughout my being the rightness in her words — even as my mind tried desperately to make it not so.

I didn't know anything about the Tasmanian Aboriginals, but others did. So all week they were filling me in about the Black Line, where the English settlers, soldiers, and prisoners made a line across Tasmania and then moved across the state to round up the natives. What a horrible idea! I learned later that it was a total failure, finding only one young boy and an old man.

I was also told that all the full-blooded Tasmanian indigenous people were gone. That they had all been killed or died. I found this deeply troubling, and wouldn't learn until years later that it wasn't true, at least not in the eyes of their descendants who are still there.

The next morning while half asleep, I remembered having a fragment of a dream. I could see an infinity symbol on its side like the number eight, and the words in my mind were: ***Infinity, held in place by the Aboriginal song into the Dreamtime.***

***

So many people shook, goose-bumped, or had given me messages that I knew I was on the right track. But the one who was most surprising and really tickled me was the guy in Whole Foods weeks later. He was offering information about a service of some kind.

"No, thanks, I'm going to Tasmania soon," I said, smiling.

"Oh my God, my toes are tingling!" he yelled after me, not realizing that he had been used as a messenger for Spirit.

It was a no-brainer. If I couldn't do what I'm here to do without going to Tasmania, then I was going. But how? My finances were stretched, cards maxed, and only a few weeks of vacation coming.

PART 2
The Journey

Chapter 8

Veronica and the Communities

When I arrived in Australia, I was filled with such great anticipation. I didn't know what I was being called for, or who was calling. And I couldn't even feel the calls, except for that vague sense of rightness I feel when I am taking the right path.

My friend Veronica in Cairns was the first stop, just to visit. I was going to Tasmania for a month, but why not visit a few of my friends while down under? I had been to Oz before, visiting the Miracles Center in Byron Bay. For five years in a row I had spent three months there, having a glorious time and connecting with lots of wonderful people.

"Hey, Suebee!" Veronica yelled across the parking lot.

"Veronica, you look great," I chirped as I rolled my bags toward her. "Thanks for picking me up."

"No worries, mate," she responded in her wonderful Aussie accent. "Let's get you home and fed and rested up. I have big plans for us tomorrow."

"Oh yeah? What are we doing?" I asked, intrigued.

"We're going to an event at one of the communities," she offered. "I spend lots of time there and I want to go support my friends."

"Ummmm, what does that mean? What kind of community?" I asked, a bit confused.

"One of the Aboriginal communities. That's what they're called. I mostly go up to visit the Cape York communities where I have some great friends. But I work one day a week at some of the local communities. It won't be anything fancy. It's just an event to bring more awareness about child abuse, but there will be dancing and all sorts of things going on. It'll be fun. Do you mind?" she quickly asked.

I was stunned. So many people had told me the Aboriginals were calling me to come, but I didn't expect to meet any of them just hours off the plane.

"Veronica, I don't mind at all, and it is beyond perfect. You have no idea how perfect."

I laughed when we reached her car. It was a Toyota Land Cruiser that was incredibly high with a snorkel that went above the roofline and an enormous bull grill on the front. I asked about the snorkel, since I'd never seen anything like it. It was in case she went through any deep water crossings. I was quite astonished by the thought, but later she showed me pictures of some of the river crossings and I understood why she needed such a rugged rig. It's not like people drive by regularly and can help you if you get in a jam. And if you're covered in water, you want your engine to get oxygen to keep running.

At her house, we had a quick meal and began catching up on each other's life — me telling her about leaving the spiritual community, traveling with Rubens Faria, the Brazilian spiritual healer who channels Dr. Fritz, getting sick, and finally being called to go to Tasmania.

And she filled me in on her life away from the Miracles Center. She was working in an emergency call center, so had many interactions with the Aboriginal communities. I remembered that she always had a deep connection with the Aboriginals — so I was happy she was now closely involved with them. She bought herself a special caravan (Aussie trailer) designed to survive the rough roads up Cape York way.

We talked as long as I could keep my eyes open, but we were getting up early. In the few minutes before I fell completely asleep, I marveled that I had just arrived in Australia and tomorrow I was going to an Aboriginal community with someone who knows them.

***

The event at the Aboriginal community was interesting for sure, and it was nice to walk around and meet her friends. I especially enjoyed watching the young boys dance because it was unlike anything I'd seen before.

But as we enjoyed the day I felt a noticeable lack of connection. These were obviously not the people I was called to Oz to meet. I pondered this as I was walking around until I finally got it.

I didn't come from the other side of the planet for Aboriginals who are alive. I came for the ones in spirit — the dead ones, I thought quietly, a bit shaken up by this realization. I was sure this is what I was being told, but I wasn't at all sure how I felt about it. I wasn't one to seek out ghosts or dead spirits. It's not that I hadn't encountered them before – I had. But it had been a bit weird how I recognized it.

It had happened four years earlier while I was driving across the US. I was caught in a blizzard in Buffalo, NY, staying at an ordinary budget hotel. I was in the bath relaxing when suddenly I looked to the door.

"You can stop watching me now!" I blurted. It really surprised me, because I hadn't been thinking anything of the sort. Yet it had popped out as if I were responding to something I'd heard or seen. It also creeped me out, so I quickly got out of the tub and into my pajamas.

Weird, I thought to myself. *All right angels, if there is someone here, please take care of me, and help them out, too, if they need it.*

With that I put it out of my mind and went off to bed, but the next day when the hotel asked me to move to another room I wasn't surprised. I felt it was a response to the previous night's prayer. It would be years before I knew how to help such discarnate beings, but at that point, it just scared me and caused me to pray.

So, inwardly knowing I was in Australia to connect with dead Aboriginals definitely gave me reason, yet again, to wonder what I was doing. And within a day, I was quite certain it wasn't dead spirits in mainland Australia, but specifically the spirits of Aboriginals in Tasmania.

Staying with Veronica for a few days was not only fun, but perfect. She showed me around the area while we caught up on all the people we knew. But even more perfect — Veronica was born and raised in Tasmania, and could fill me in on both the state and the indigenous people there.

I pulled out the book Hart had insisted I bring with me, *Voices of the First Day*, by Robert Lawlor. It arrived just hours before I left Oregon, and I was almost a bit sorry. It was a large, heavy book for a backpacking traveler. I didn't know at the time, but this book would be a key player in the unfolding of my adventure. Oh, how I was underestimating grace!

"Have you ever seen this book, Veronica?" I asked as I took it out of my backpack and laid it on the day bed.

"I don't know. Let me have a look. Oh, this looks interesting," she mumbled as she flipped some pages. "Some really old pics of the Aborigines. They don't like being called that, you know."

"Oh, no, I didn't know, but I don't think I've called them much of anything so far. They've never been on my radar, so it was quite surprising when they showed up in my meditations at the Mystery School."

"Huh? What's a mystery school?"

So I filled her in on my epiphany on New Year's Day and how quickly the Universe responded by sending me to the Miracles Mastery Workshop.

"That's where I first heard Jean Houston, and was just flabbergasted. I had a whole download that weekend, and was signed up for her Mystery School before Sunday. It's been a great experience meeting all these amazing women. Most of them are older than us and have been doing this for up to twenty five years. But they are all artists and activists and freethinkers for sure.

"All the weekends have been great. But it was the one in May, they call the Gifting, where Jean goes into a kind of trance and grants you a wish. That's the one that probably set this trip in motion."

"Really? What did you wish for?" Veronica asked, looking up from the book.

"I asked for fertile ground. It's what popped into my head while I was driving there. I was thinking about wanting to bloom or blossom or flourish. And it just seemed like I needed fertile ground. I certainly didn't have that working as an accountant for the county." We laughed out loud.

"So it was about six weeks later when I went to the week-long Mystery School summer program. I met an amazing woman from Australia who offered to do a future life regression," I said, wondering why it's not called a progression.

"That sounds interesting Sue. How'd it go?" Veronica plied.

"At first I was worried because I'm a rock. In guided meditations, when they say go here and see this, I never see anything. I never feel anything. So I was worried the regression would be like that once again."

By now Veronica had laid down the book and was listening intently. "Yeah, go on! I wanna hear what happened!"

"Well, it was a really deep hypnosis — I couldn't move. She took me forward to different points in time, but I couldn't see anything."

"Oh, Sue, I bet you were frustrated."

"No, actually, I wasn't feeling frustrated, I just figured it was the same as always. I was just hoping she was getting something," I offered. "So finally she brought me out of hypnosis and said that something was missing. Because she couldn't see anything either."

"Oh, no, how long ago was that?" she blurted and laughed. "Are you going to die while you're here?" Veronica looked both amused and concerned.

"Well," I paused to think. "That would have been three months ago. And yes, that possibility did cross my mind, although she didn't think it was that. She felt that I needed to find something before I could know or see where I was headed."

"Man, that would have freaked me right out! I'm glad it wasn't me." Veronica laughed in her normal boisterous way.

"Well, I wasn't gonna just stop at that. So after the week, I called my friend Hart, the healer who saved my life a few years ago. She agreed that something was missing and felt it was a place. Turns out it's Tasmania.

"Finally I asked her — if I don't go to Tasmania, can I still fulfill my life's purpose?" I paused, remembering the moment again.

"Well? What did she say?"

"Her answer was a quick and simple: 'no.'"

I went on to tell Veronica all the messages I was being given in the following weeks, including the guy in the grocery store with tingling toes.

"His toes were tingling! How funny is that?" Veronica laughed.

"So here I am, on the verge of something. Yet I really don't know what I'm doing or where I'll be going in Tasmania," I added quietly as the reality sunk in.

"Oh, Sue, you're going to have a great time, especially if you stop saying Tasmania and just start calling it Tassie." She smiled as she started pulling off a layer. "Tassie is so beautiful and not at all like the mainland. For one, it isn't so bloody hot!"

"Veronica, something sort of strange came up after the call with Hart." I started slowly, wondering if I should share this part.

"Yeah, come on then. Tell me," she encouraged.

"Well, I was meditating one day and asking why I was going to Tasmania, I mean Tassie." I laughed as I caught myself. "You have to know this has been such a massive turn in my path, and

I was both excited and scared. I knew I didn't have the money for this trip, and then . . ." I paused again, deciding whether to go on.

"So what did you find out?" she quizzed.

"I was told, in that subtle way I know things, that I was going to Tasmania . . ." I paused to let the words surface in my awareness. ". . . To embrace the galactic formulating consciousness of the earth and its inhabitants and bring it into awareness." As I voiced those words, I felt the pull within me to a place of deep and ancient knowing.

"Whoa!" she exclaimed. "That sounds big. What does it mean exactly? Any idea?"

"Well, yeah, and not really." I chuckled before continuing. "I don't know what it means exactly, but somewhere deep within me I *know*. I can feel a deep recognition that knows exactly what I'm up to. I just wish that deep knowing would fill me in." I groaned and could feel my exasperation.

I've always hated that things are so understated for me. Everyone else gets clear guidance in words, in visions; but for me, it's always very subtle. Somewhere along the way I had to make peace with the fact that I'm obviously wired differently. There must be a reason I've yet to discover. Once in a channeling session, the guides asked me if I wanted them to slow down the words so I could actually hear them. I understood what they were saying and I love efficiency, so it never occurred to me to say yes.

"Bloody hell, Sue. Sounds like it's gonna be quite the adventure! You'll have to let me know what happens."

Veronica went back to looking at the book while I sat and pondered. I was still feeling some jet lag, so knew I'd be going to bed a bit early.

"Hey, look at this, Sue. There's a whole chapter in this book on the Tasmanian Aboriginals. That's so interesting. I can't wait to hear what he has to say."

"I'm fading fast, Veronica. I'm going to have to sleep now. You let me know what you find out in the morning," I yawned as I crawled into bed.

"Righteo!" Her voice trailed off as she took the book and headed down the hall.

I'm finally here in Australia. Tasmania is just four weeks away. Hmmmmm — I hope I find out why I'm here. I hope it's not just another subtle journey.

Chapter 9

Setups and Stumbles

Now that I was heading toward Tasmania, I could feel an undercurrent of something unknown, yet still feeling the sense of rightness in some way. It felt like preparations were happening — but how or for what eluded me.

Occasionally I would get a glimpse or be aware of the set-up. Like arriving at a friend's house down the coast for a few days and discovering a copy of Dan Brown's book, *The Da Vinci Code.* I knew the book was wildly popular, but I wasn't much of a book reader, and never read novels. Yet the need to read it was undeniable, so I picked it up and dove in. I had a real sense of dropping deeper into the rabbit hole regarding the Illuminati and the men with the power and money. I had clearly asked the question about why my tribe was like a pack of locusts on the earth, and this felt like part of the answer being given me — a piece to the puzzle.

Another divine insertion was when I was having lunch with several old friends in Buderim, sharing my travels and catching up on their lives. Just a day before, Judy had seen a video where the Aboriginals talked about welcoming the white brother

71

because all their stories told that there was something that the white tribe was meant to bring. They were waiting for the white brother to bring his 'part' to the table for the good of the earth and everyone.

I found this both interesting and surprising, since so far in history we, the white European tribe, have managed to decimate almost every indigenous population on the planet. And considering how we are treating the earth, we are probably going to destroy ourselves as well. So I started to wonder in earnest – what is it that the white tribe is meant to be bringing, and is it happening, or held up in some way?

More unexpected preparations occurred during that lunch when I had a check-in call with Hart. The conversation was quite surprising . . .

"Sue, I keep getting that date, Oct 8, when you need to be on that island, what's it called? I've been asking, but can't figure out why you need to be there on that specific day. I usually don't get dates, so it's quite unusual," Hart mused.

"Hunter Island," I filled in. "There's nothing on Hunter Island, so I don't know how I'm going to get there. I've been looking on the internet, and it's a private island. There's no public access, even though there is an Aboriginal cave there. The only people on the net who seem to go there are kayakers. I suppose I could do that." We both chuckled.

"That makes sense about the cave, Sue, I'm not surprised. I was feeling you needed to approach Tasmania from the same direction as the first Aboriginals, who came across the land bridge there." Hart always trusted her guidance, no matter what the research says.

It was fairly standard "knowledge" that the Aboriginals had migrated from mainland Australia across a land bridge on the eastern side of Tassie, not the west, as Hart was suggesting.

"I can feel the energy moving into Tasmania from there — it's like the mouth in some way. Then it moves through the island and comes out on that eastern land bridge," she continued. "It's important you get to that island on the 8th, Sue. Have you got any ideas what you're gonna do?"

"Yeah, Hart. Three Hummock Island is nearby and it takes visitors and has a caretaker. I figured I'd call them and see what they know."

"That's a great idea, I'd do that. There must be some way to get there, or I wouldn't be feeling such a strong pull." Then she added, "It's a window of opportunity into consciousness — possibly your star home, or something else I can't pinpoint. The Universe is really supporting this and will put the wind at your back. But you may not know how until you get there."

"Sue, what's going on in the middle of your head?" Her question surprised me.

"Um, I don't know. I've been feeling lots of pressure there — almost white hot. I just figured it was a headache from the jet fumes or something. Been feeling it since I landed here."

"Can you go someplace quiet and tune in? There's definitely some new activity going on there," Hart suggested.

I excused myself from the table and went to a quiet place at the side of the restaurant. "Okay, I'm in the trees." I hoped my friends wouldn't mind me deserting them, but I could feel that feeling. The one that always indicates something important was coming up. It's like a slowing down of time and space — being surrounded by pause.

"Okay, let's try a couple of things. Michael and I have been working a lot with infinity symbols lately, and you've been dreaming about them. Why don't you put one in the middle of your head and see if that relieves the pressure." Hart was always full of amazing ideas.

"Okay — doing that," I said slowly, concentrating on the infinity symbol. "Oh, it seems to want to spin. Is that okay?" I was hoping she would say yes, because my attempts to stop it seemed useless.

"Yeah, Sue, that should be okay. Just give it a minute and see what happens."

"Oh, my gosh!" I was speechless as I felt the symbol moving.

"What's happening, Sue?"

"Uh, it started to spin faster and faster and then it began gyrating — you know, like a gyroscope. And boy, my head feels so much better — I can't believe it. Thanks, Hart. I thought I was gonna have to travel with that." Hart never ceased to amaze me with how she knew what to recommend.

"That's great, Sue. I can see it's definitely shifting the stuckness that was there. You may have to use that a few times during your trip to stay clear."

Three years ago when I was so very sick, I was quite certain that she saved my life and my sanity. But I was always in awe of how she could so deeply know and feel things. She could muscle test anything just by feeling in her own body. But her abilities were downright otherworldly — beyond psychic, beyond intuitive. Such deep knowing and integrity.

***

I spent the next couple of days trying to find a way to Hunter Island. I could see blog posts from the kayakers who had paddled by the island, but the Base Strait is notoriously treacherous water.

Kayaking will have to be my last resort. I chuckled at the thought and figured if I tried that it would be my last everything.

Finally, I discovered how to contact the caretakers on Three Hummock Island, the next island over from Hunter. They occasionally allowed visitors so I gave them a call and talked to a really nice woman, Jane. I explained my dilemma and she gave me the name of a pilot who could fly in and out of these islands. I was so grateful and excited.

Next I called the pilot, who was only too happy to take on the job. But he said that Hunter was a leased island and I should get permission from the leaseholder for him to land. Fortunately, he was able to give me the guy's number.

I was feeling lucky as I had stumbled upon a way to get there — not an easy feat. So I was surprised when I called the leaseholder. He was nice enough, but said the landing strip was under water, and there was no way the pilot would be able to land there. And besides, there were 300 head of feral cows on the island that would most certainly charge me if I went there.

Feeling suddenly deflated, I called the pilot to give him the news and ask him if he had any other ideas. He didn't.

Usually when I run into a brick wall with something I'm trying to do, I just assume I'm not meant to do it and go to Plan B. But this time was different somehow. It felt so meant-to-be that I decided to keep trying — even though I was out of ideas. I rang Jane again and asked if there were any other options.

"Oh yeah, you can always take a boat over," Jane said casually. "We go over to mainland Tassie once a month to get supplies. Just call Terry in Smithton. Just a tic. I've got his number right here somewhere." I was profusely grateful and couldn't wait to give Terry a ring.

"Hi, Terry, this is Sue. Jane on Three Hummock gave me your number. She says you take people and supplies out there. Any chance to book a ride out to Hunter Island on October 8?" I paused and held my breath.

"Hi, Sue. Yeah, right. Well, uh, I do take people and cargo out there, but it's not the best time of year to be going there. The winds are bloody horrible at the minute." The silence following his statement was deafening.

Finally, I pressed on. "Terry, could we say maybe and just watch the weather as it gets closer? You must get an occasional break in the weather, don't you?" I was shamelessly grasping for a shred of hope.

"Yeah, well, uh. Sure, we could do that. Why don't you call me a bit closer, maybe a few days before? Yeah?" He was hesitant to say that, I could tell, but I decided to just focus on the words that spoke of a possibility.

"Great. Thanks so much, Terry. I'll call you a few days before and see how it's going. You take care." The enthusiasm in my voice was a little over the top. Even I could see through it.

Two days later I got a short email from Hart . . .

"Sue, while I was washing dishes, I finally got why you need to be on Hunter Island on October 8. A galactic portal is opening that day. – Hart."

Chapter 10

Messages from Colin's Toilet

Now, this should have been good news to have the mystery solved, but it wasn't. I'm not a galactic kind of girl, so this definitely gave me reason to pause.

What the hell am I doing? A galactic portal? What the frig am I going to do with a galactic portal? My mind was racing. I couldn't even dream up a scenario of what meeting a galactic portal was going to be like. Forget that worst-case scenario game! It was even worse than having a white witch wake me up 20 years earlier! I had a frame of reference about a witch, good or bad, but a galactic portal? Obviously I wasn't a sci-fi fan or I might have been excited.

So now that I had a "maybe" to get to the island, I was praying lots, in between wondering what to say to a galactic portal. I mean, psychics and channelers are one thing, even spirits and ghosts I can do — maybe — but a galactic portal was a bit of a stretch.

Obviously the Universe sensed my concern . . .

***

I was staying with my friend Colin for a few days in Buderim before I was to leave for Tassie. Colin is renowned for being a very funny guy with a loud, infectious laugh. He always brought a bit of levity to the spiritual community where we met. We spent the first couple of days laughing, as we went to the beach and I shared the details of my journey. Then on the third morning I had a very unusual experience.

Colin was already up having his breakfast when I stumbled out from the toilet.

"Colin! I just had the strangest experience!"

"You just got up, what's so strange?" he asked.

"I was sitting on the toilet minding my own business, when I realized that — the galactic portal was aware of me." I sat down at the table with my head in my hands.

"Really!?" Colin laughed, looking up from his breakfast.

"And the weird thing is — I can't even tell you how I knew. I was just aware of it. It was up here above me," I motioned above my right shoulder. "And it was aware of me.

"Colin, I've been very uncomfortable about this galactic portal thing. It's definitely not something I've ever aspired to — having a date with a galactic portal."

"What are you worried about? What could go wrong? I hear only the nicest people frequent galactic portals," Colin snickered. "Are you worried about what to wear? Or what you'll say?" Colin laughed, cereal falling out of his mouth. "And what if you don't recognize it and start talking to empty space? I'm sure it'll be very offended!" That visual got us both howling.

"You're right," I continued. "I have no idea what a galactic portal looks like, or even if it looks like anything. I've been wondering if I was going to meet some strange beings or feel some weird energy. Or be beamed up or something worse. I can't even imagine what I'll find there. Talk about out of my comfort zone."

We sat quietly for a few moments as I felt around in my mind for more recollections of what I had just experienced.

"No, seriously, Sue, what did it feel like? What were you thinking? Were you embarrassed it was watching you pee?" Colin's seriousness level was slightly challenged.

"No, I wasn't embarrassed. It didn't occur to me to be embarrassed. But as I sat there on the toilet I was filled with a wonderfully warm, comforting feeling."

"Warm, comforting feeling while you're peeing? What's so unusual about that?" Colin joked, causing me to grimace.

"No, Colin, I don't mean the warm feeling was from peeing! It was one of those warm feelings that starts at the top of your head and feels like you're melting and softening. That kind of feeling when you're filled with light and peace and stillness, like slipping into eternity. It was so sweet I wanted to just dissolve or wrap up in it. And then I realized I wasn't afraid anymore. The galactic portal doesn't feel scary, it feels . . . almost loving.

"I also felt something else, like some sort of tractor beam was put on me. Not one that's pulling or manipulating me, just connecting to me. It feels like it might be helping me get there — like I'll be able to make it to Hunter Island now."

"That's great Sue! I didn't realize my toilet was a direct line to anything important. Maybe it's a little portal all its own. Not galactic or anything," Colin got up to clear his dishes.

"I'm not sure it's your toilet in particular, Colin. It's amazing how often I have a great flash of clarity while I'm sitting on the toilet. Do you know what I mean? I don't know what it is about the toilet that is conducive to such intuitive revelations. Maybe just taking a minute for a release of sorts allows more openness."

"Yeah, I've had those moments too!" Colin agreed. So for the next hour we howled and compared our best toilet revelations. And for the rest of my visit, every time I came out of a toilet, Colin would ask, "Any messages?"

Chapter 11

Cliff Ahead ~
Preparing to Jump

Within two weeks of discovering Tasmania as "the missing piece", I gave a month's notice at work. That would give me time to get things in order both at work and at home.

Hart initially had suggested I go to Tasmania for five months, which was beyond my ability to imagine. I was quitting my job, so I would have the time, but the money necessary seemed impossible. If it wasn't for my vacation pay, I wouldn't be going at all. So I planned on three months: a month in Tasmania and a month on either side to see my Aussie friends.

I was well aware that often during my travels I would get involved in life and delay returning "home." So rather than leaving my RV in the campground for an uncertain amount of time, I went about winterizing it to put it in storage.

My biggest concern was Percy. I couldn't stand the idea of putting him back into the pet hotel for such a long time. It was a great place, but it wasn't fair to him. So I started praying.

If you need me to go to Tasmania, you have to find Percy a better home than mine! Someone who loves him more and takes fantastic care of him. I was teary as I also prayed to the kitty angels.

Percy and I had had quite a journey together. When I found him in a shelter a year ago, he was the most beautiful kitty I had ever seen — a long-haired Siamese of sorts with crystal blue eyes and incredibly soft cappuccino fur. Only one problem: he would nip me if I stroked him beyond his shoulders. I was patient and kind, but even after two months, he would still nip. One day a visiting psychic friend said he had been abused and did Reiki on his hip area. From then on he was happy to be petted and never nipped again.

We did surprisingly well living in such a small space. We were too close to the highway to let him out, so he would chase the feathered wand up and down the aisle for exercise. Otherwise, he would sit at the window, watching life go by. Eventually we moved to a wooded campground with lots of space and no traffic. He was so happy to be outside again, and would often bring me "presents."

The breakthrough came when I went into the UPS office where I received my mail to tell them I would be leaving in a month. I also mentioned that my kitty would need a new home if they knew anyone looking for one. Well, the woman working there started jumping up and down and said she wanted a new kitty. She already had two, but her boyfriend promised her she could have another. I showed her his picture and she was in love.

A week later she came to pick him up. It was a bittersweet moment for me. I was so sad to say goodbye to my dear friend, whom I loved. He had been such a blessing to me. But I was also so happy for him as I watched her petting him all the way down his back. He was not afraid, he didn't nip, and he was now a great pet.

On my last trip to the UPS office I got the update. He could go in and out as he pleased and became boss kitty. Every night he would sit on her lap to be petted. I was sad, but so grateful that the kitty angels had found him a wonderful home full of love.

***

I was spending my last two days in Oregon at the beach, when I received a sign — a blessing — that let me know I was definitely on the right track. I was just walking on the beach in the surf, enjoying the beautiful sunny day when something unexpected happened.

I had been cursed in Belize by three women practicing black magic some 20 years earlier. They had caused three open oozing sores on my legs that grew at an alarming speed until the Mayan shaman gave me a powerful remedy. The sores healed, but the curses had remained — many psychics could see them and many healers had attempted to remove them, to no avail. I hadn't thought of them in years, and somehow had managed to keep moving forward on my path in spite of their attempt "to not let me walk with grace on the earth."

As I walked the beach, I suddenly *knew* "they" were gone. The curses had been swept away by that gentle wave that splashed my feet. I was stunned. But I knew it was true — they were gone. I knew this was an auspicious sign that I was indeed on the right track.

Chapter 12

On the Right Track

I went to the symposium, I signed up for Jean Houston's Mystery School, and I let my mind run free and crazy with the remembrance of being an alchemist. I knew I was finally on the right track — heading in the right direction. I knew if I would go to the Mystery School weekends, something in my life would shift. I did expect it to move a little quicker than it did, but I also underestimated what a monumental shift it would be.

Ever since my spiritual awakening I have been surrounded by friends with various gifts of clairvoyance, clairaudience, psychic abilities, and such. For years, maybe decades, I found it frustrating to have to make decisions without access to this information from a higher perspective. I would have loved to give away my right to decide in order to be assured of the best outcome.

That old perfectionist in me was always trying to do it right and be perfect. It took a long time for me to realize that some of my issues to try and heal in this life were actually to give up trying to be perfect and being a good girl all the time. I had lifetimes of giving my power away, of submitting to spiritual authority, of deferring to someone else's decisions. So a big lesson for me this time around was having to make choices and decisions for myself — therefore having the decision made for me was not going to be a useful thing.

And yet when I looked at my life, I could see that there definitely was something guiding me and helping me. In fact, if I didn't get in the way, I would stumble into way more grace and blessings than if I were trying to run the show.

This has been very confusing to me for most of my life as I tried to balance making choices for myself with also being open to divine guidance, direction, and inspiration. But there's a big difference between deciding what is "right" or "best" and then trying to get Reality to agree with you — or allowing Reality to unfold gracefully with some input and choices from you.

I had to learn to pay careful attention to what I felt in my gut and heart, not just my mind. And also to watch the signs, the synchronicities, the help flowing my way.

I believe that you can *feel* it when you're on the right track. It's such a deep sense of rightness about your life and what's going on. And likewise, you can *feel* it when you're lost, when you're heading the wrong direction, or when you've bitten off more than you can chew. You know the moments.

Sometimes I've overlooked that sense of wrongness just because it wasn't what I wanted to hear. I asked guidance once about why I wasn't told about the breakup of my relationship sooner. The answer was very clear — I was being told, but I didn't listen because I didn't want it to be true.

What I love more than anything is when I can feel *grace* moving with me. Where it is guiding me and helping me to see the signs I need to see. Where there's a flow and the direction is obvious, and things just fall into place. Or where some things are almost repelled if they don't belong. That's the best feeling ever.

One of the worst feelings is when you *know* you've missed the wave — missed that divinely orchestrated opportunity to move forward on your path with ease and grace. You can feel the energy shift when it happens, and you know that the road coming to meet you will be fraught with challenges. Or worse yet, you'll feel dead in the water and unable to move, completely uncertain how to proceed. I have been in this place before, and waiting for the next wave to come round, or for Plan B to be formulated by the Universe, can seem like forever. You feel like you're standing still and treading water — because you are.

When I'm having this experience, all I know to do is to hang in there, align with my Divine Self, and ask for help – lots of help. When I've missed a wave, it's always because I was afraid: to make the leap into something new, to embrace something being offered, to get out of my comfort zone.

I try not to beat myself up, just make the best use of the down-time and be ready, really ready, when the next wave or opportunity comes. The comfort zone won't win next time around, for sure.

I have found that watching for signs will usually tell me how things are going. If things surface and fall into place easily, I'm probably on the right track. Or if things feel like there's no energy, kind of clunky or impossible, like I'm trying to push the river — that's when I step back and see if I'm trying to have things "my way" or if I've missed the opportunity.

When I'm trying to make something happen, it's an obvious sign I'm too invested in the outcome and not open to divine timing or grace. I have at times known what was coming and tried to force it to hurry rather than waiting for it to ripen and fall from the tree of its own accord. I can be so impatient, so I try not to worry, and just step back and let grace catch up.

We all have access to grace, I'm certain of it. Grace is a field of energy that can be accessed, but not on your own terms. It takes relaxing, melting, dissolving into the field — letting grace permeate you and your life. We've all had those moments when you feel like you're traveling with ease and nothing can go wrong — those times when you're not trying to dictate the future but just going with the flow and letting things unfold naturally. Those are the grace-filled moments.

Grace is interesting because you can't use it to get your way. As soon as I get into a frame of mind where I want things to be "my way," grace disappears and things get chunky again. As I learned all these lessons, I was opened up to more grace and a gentler unfolding. It was through grace that I gathered the courage to follow my journey — no matter how strange it appeared as it unfolded before me.

I know it takes courage to move forward and to be open to the journey of the evolving self. Yet it is the journey we each came to travel. We each have something wondrous to share with the world and each other. And if any of us allows ourself to express our divine essence in whatever way we are called, we give everyone else permission to do the same. The more we all embrace our real selves, the happier we are. This affects everyone around us and certainly affects the whole world.

Chapter 13

Going Beyond Forgiveness

It was during a nine-year stint in a spiritual community that I dove deeply into A Course in Miracles. This book was a Godsend. It gave me the guidance to really delve deeply into my own mind, my heart, and the nature of reality. That book and its wisdom from Jesus became foundational to my being.

During that process of deepening my connection with the Divine, I really came to *know* that the Universe, God, Creation, whatever you call it, is a single, whole reality with nothing in opposition. By its nature of being whole, there is nothing outside of it. It is also wholly beneficent and benevolent.

Knowing this brought me great peace, and also enabled me to remember that everything is in harmony. It taught me how to move with grace in the world and to receive both grace and miracles in my life.

If the Universe is whole and benevolent, then it is not possible to be a victim of anything. But it is possible to make some really bad choices and suffer the effects of these. Karma is a really bad idea, and it's time for us to choose something different.

Breaking Agreements

The famous quote attributed to Gandhi, **an eye for an eye makes the whole world blind,** is so very true.

When I discovered I could break the agreement with the other soul group to pass the torture baton back and forth, I could tell it was no longer carried with me — either in my mind or my body. I could also feel it unravel the baggage for the other soul group.

At the time I didn't realize what had happened, except that I was free. I didn't think any more about it until it started showing up in my awareness with other memories, especially with the prisoners. That's when I started really asking questions and when the answers started seeping in.

I was shown how we make these awful agreements while we are still in spirit. We have no idea what they will feel like when we're inhabiting a body, as either the victim or the perpetrator. We honor these agreements because we are honorable, and suffer terribly. And when we die and return to spirit, we don't remember how unspeakable these events felt to us. And yet we continue to carry the effects of these horrific agreements for lifetimes.

Each time we return to a new life, we have all our emotional baggage to deal with, to try to clear and resolve. It's how it was set up, but it's obvious that something's not working well. We seem to be digging ourselves into a deeper and deeper hole. You may not recognize it personally if you're having a good life this time through, but look at humanity.

And karma, once started, just keeps cycling around and reverberates through the eons. I hurt you, you hurt me, over and over and over and over and over . . . *Enough already!*

It always blows me away when people defend pain and suffering, saying it's necessary. I agree that challenges and competition are necessary for us to learn and grow. But there is a culture, a paradigm of cruelty and suffering inflicted on another, that is not necessary — that is not even natural. But we defend the idea because it's too upsetting to think that all our pain and suffering was pointless or unnecessary.

People often struggle with the idea of forgiveness. So when you talk about unraveling the perpetrator's karma, that's just going too far. Yet it's such a freeing thing to do — to break the agreements, to clear the karma for both sides. I was so very aware that we never know who we've been or what we've done in other lifetimes. We don't know if we were wronged initially or as payback for what we did to another. We all want to believe we were important or did not participate in the horrific chapters in history. And yet if you could remember all your lifetimes, I'm guessing we would all remember some lives when we were the bad guy, the one who maimed or raped.

We've tried out all the roles, good and bad. Frankly, it's time to drop some of these agreements rather than continue to recycle them. When will we have learned enough is enough?

How Does Breaking the Agreement Unravel Karma?

It took me a while to figure this out. I had already broken the first torture agreement and knew it had cleared, but didn't know how.

Eventually I remembered back to a book I read after my awakening. It was about many metaphysical things, including karma and reincarnation. Things I knew nothing about, and yet when I read the chapter, I remembered that I did know those things in some deep and ancient part of me.

So when I got to the chapters on time and space I was shocked to realize that I also knew these things deeply within me. I could feel profoundly that time is a construct and the only time there is — is right now. Yesterday and tomorrow are never here, not ever — just our ideas about them. We believe we are moving through time, but there is absolutely no proof that that is true. It's only us believing a construct that we as humans have all agreed to believe to make this journey plausible.

And even space is something constructed and held as true. However, if you go inside your own mind, all you can know is you. Only you. Only here. And only now. When you move through the world, you are always here. Nowhere else. I flew into New Zealand once and was thrilled to be there. Yet, when the plane landed I looked out the window and suddenly knew — it's still me right here. I have a new story of being in New Zealand, so I'll believe it, but it's still just me right here.

It was when I was shown about the prisoners being ready now. I knew I didn't want to go talk to the prisoners every few months to keep things clear for them. So it came to me to leave the invitation outside of time and space. They could get to it whenever they're ready. My invitation didn't need to remain in our customary ideas of time and space — it could be eternally available.

That's when I realized that when I originally broke the agreement for my village to be tortured, I was outside of time and space. How do I know? Because my body was lying on a bed in Shutesbury, MA in 2001, and I was acutely aware of something taking place somewhere else — probably during the middle ages. And yet when I broke the agreement, I was relieved, noticeably relieved, in that body on my friend's bed.

And since that time, as I've worked with hundreds of clients, I've seen the emotional baggage they've been carrying dissolve from their faces, their bodies, their minds when they break the agreements that caused their suffering, even when it was from lifetimes ago.

Unraveling Karma for the Collective

During the months following the revelations about the prisoners, some unusual things started to occur. I would happen across a story that was horrific to me in some way — about slavery or torture, sexual trafficking, or child abuse — even organ harvesting. The story would haunt me for days until I realized that I was being asked to go into the unconscious human collective and invite those souls involved to break the agreements to suffer and cause suffering.

This was certainly *not* what I expected to be called to do, so I was quite reluctant. But the nudging was so persistent that I finally listened, and would look intensely into the depths of each situation. Connecting with souls on both sides of these situations gave me a whole different perspective. And what was unfolding in the process was a deep understanding of how agreements and karma have fueled all the cruelty and suffering in this world.

I was very skeptical about these experiences and knowings that were coming to me, so I didn't mention them to anyone. I had no way to prove to myself that anything was happening, and frankly, I wondered if I was losing it. Yet if I'd stop and do the work, I would feel tremendous relief and they would stop hovering around me. Occasionally I would ask for a really clear sign so I'd stop doubting myself, and the signs would always come.

Eventually I mentioned something about it to Hart to see if I was nuts. I knew that Hart would not hesitate to let me know if I was delusional. (She was very grounded and not the least bit airy-fairy.) She would listen to my story, and assure me that I was not crazy. In fact, she was quite intrigued with what I was encountering and definitely felt I was on the right track.

Chapter 14
Spirit of Tasmania

I flew to Melbourne to catch the SPIRIT OF TASMANIA, the ferry that would take me to Tassie. I had known weeks earlier that I needed to travel slowly across the Bass Strait for some reason, so that meant using the ferry rather than flying. It almost felt like I had a date with destiny, whether it meant I would meet someone on the crossing or something else.

I had booked the trip online and had some choices. It's an overnight voyage of ten hours, so there's going to be a price to pay, in either money or lack of sleep. The cabins were expensive, so I opted for an "ocean view recliner." I was pretty good at sleeping anywhere.

The thought of meeting a galactic portal was no longer troubling. I felt a sort of comfort with it now, as if it were guiding me and traveling with me to keep me safe. I didn't know how that works. And I was feeling that the grace I was traveling with would somehow get me to Hunter Island on the appointed date. Grace had led me to the fisherman with the boat, so certainly grace could calm the winds for the crossing.

My only concern was a very worried email I had received from my friend, Jackie. She had a bad feeling about me going on the boat with Terry, the fisherman, and was almost begging me not to do it. I deeply considered her warning because I had, on several occasions during this trip, felt the sensation of traveling in big water with enormous waves — and of gently floating down to the bottom of the sea. This was a sensation that did not create fear in me, but I was well aware that it had surfaced several times now. So when I got Jackie's email, I wondered if this was my time to leave the planet. I wasn't afraid of death, but it did make me wonder.

Crossing the Bass Strait

It was dusk when I finally walked into the ferry terminal. Visiting friends had been great, but I had finally reached the beginning of my real journey and I was beyond excited.

I was a bit early, but there were so few people around, I wondered if I would have the whole ferry to myself. As I checked in, I was hoping for a great seat — so was happy when I was assigned a front-row recliner. Little did I know what a set-up this would turn out to be.

After checking my bags, I walked onto the boat to find a nice-looking man in a ferry shirt standing there.

I juggled things while I pulled out my boarding pass and asked, "Are you going to tell me where to go?"

"Well, I can," he responded, and we laughed. He looked at my pass and pointed to the right. "You'll find the ocean-view recliners down there."

I found my way to my front-row recliner, which was right next to the muster door facing a wall. *No worries*, I thought, *it'll be dark and I'll be sleeping.* Then I saw the sign saying no baggage in front of the door. I looked around but couldn't find a place to put my carry-on bags. Certainly I wasn't expected to hold the laptop and food bag for the entire ten-hour trip.

Other people had started to arrive and settle in. They didn't seem to have the baggage problem, in fact, they didn't seem to have any bags. That's when I realized they must have brought their cars. No wonder the terminal was so empty.

I decided to go find Reception to ask what to do. I headed out into the hallway, and ran into the same nice-looking man. He recognized me and asked, "Did you find the lounge?"

"Yes, I found it, but I'm right next to the muster door and it says no baggage in front of the door. They told me to bring my laptop with me, but now I don't know what to do with it. I really don't want to hold it the whole trip," I said, wondering if he thought I was just a complaining American.

"Well, after the ship takes off, come down to the restaurant and find me and I'll see if we can get you a cabin," he offered. My mouth hung open and I could barely believe my ears. My new best friend!

I returned to my seat in disbelief, still in a daze at the possibility of a cabin. After a disappointing forage in my food bag, I grabbed my laptop bag and started to wander around the ferry exploring.

When I made it to the main deck, I was shocked to see the bar and restaurants swarming with people. *Where did all these people come from?* I wondered as I squeezed through the crowd.

When I reached the outside deck, I could see the long line of vehicles still waiting to be loaded. Not only passenger cars, but an assortment of tractor-trailers carrying building supplies, livestock, and everything else imaginable. Obviously everyone flies unless they're taking their car or transporting goods — or having a date with destiny.

I continued wandering around looking for the upper outside decks. *There are so many passages, you could easily get lost.* I thought as I reached the top of some stairs. The door opened and out came my new best friend.

"You have the timing of a gypsy," he said, obviously surprised to run into me here. "Just come find me after we get under way and I'll see about a cabin."

"Okay." I went to continue on my way and realized he'd come out of an authorized staff-only door.

How weird. No wonder he was surprised to see me. The timing of a gypsy, wonder what that means. I turned around and continued to explore the ship.

The gift shop was packed with people, so I moved onto the tourist information office, which might actually be helpful. If I was going to reach Hunter Island on time, I would have to figure out how to get to Smithton to meet the fisherman. According to the guidebook, you can't get there from here unless you have a car.

The guidebook said the logging trucks make the narrow roads very harrowing for foreign travelers, so I hadn't really considered renting a car. I had driven on the left a few years ago, but didn't really want to practice while dodging logging trucks. So instead I had a strange schedule of bus possibilities that head in the Smithton direction, but don't really go there. Hitchhiking would be my fallback position, but I was hoping for some divine intervention here. So with hope in my heart, I waited to ask the agent about other possibilities.

The passenger before me was getting information about rental cars, so I overheard that Hertz had a special deal at the moment. It was actually a reasonable price, much lower than I'd been quoted earlier.

When my turn came I was disappointed to find the guidebook was right. The bus doesn't run on Sunday. Monday's bus goes in the afternoon. Or you can rent a car. She was nice enough, but offered no other options. I walked away thinking about the situation. To reach Hunter Island on October 8, I needed to get to Smithton Sunday night. But the thought of renting a car still scared me.

So after all the vehicles were loaded (and by then a lot of the passengers looked loaded too), we finally pulled away from the dock and headed out to open water. Melbourne receded into one long glimmering string of lights, and somewhere to the east there were fireworks. A celebration for my departure, I was sure. As the lights faded away, I started to shiver. The night was chilly and the wind quickly made it unbearable. We were finally under way, so I headed to the restaurant to look for my friend.

I found him bussing tables and emptying trash cans. He certainly didn't look like a busboy, he looked like he ran the place. When he saw me, he didn't say anything, just motioned for me to follow him into the next lounge.

Stopping, he pointed to an empty chair. "You'll have to wait here. I'll need your boarding pass." I dug out my pass and handed it to him silently. "I'll be right back." He turned and walked off.

He came back a few minutes later with my boarding pass and a key. Amazing *grace*.

"All right, follow me." He turned quickly and headed out of the lounge. I was so happy to be getting a cabin, and wondered if I would be sharing. We reached the end of the long corridor and turned into another.

"By the way, my name is Peter." He had spoken so little that this surprised me.

"Hi, I'm Sue." As he led me down another corridor, I started to wonder if I was getting myself into a compromising situation. My naiveté had gotten me in trouble before.

Finally he stopped at a door. "This is it, number 314," he said as he unlocked the door. I was a little apprehensive as I followed him in. He switched on the main cabin light as I heard the door swing closed behind me. I looked around and didn't see any other personal belongings.

"The upper berth can be latched out of the way to give you more room," he said as he demonstrated.

"Here's the en suite. The lights are here." He opened the door and flicked the switch. I could see a very compact bathroom complete with shower.

"Enjoy the crossing," he said as he handed me my key and boarding pass. Then he quickly headed for the door.

"Peter, thank you so much for this! You're an angel," I called out as I followed him into the hall. He disappeared down the corridor before it even occurred to me to give him a tip. But he hadn't even paused as if he was expecting one.

I went back inside my private cabin and stared out the window. Thinking back to the Spirit of Tasmania website, I quickly realized this is their most expensive cabin . . . Four berths, en suite and large picture window — and I have it to myself!

I can't believe I opted for the cheap seats and got upgraded to this. What made him do this for me? Did he get a whisper from the Universe saying, "Peter, see that gray-haired lady over there? Please take care of her." I'm laughing at the idea. *Sue, I can't believe you were questioning the intentions of the cabin angel!*

I suddenly felt a rush of gratitude and I started to tear up. I *knew* the Universe just said a big YES to this adventure. God loves me — and Peter, my cabin angel.

It was midnight when I crawled into bed. My pajamas were in my luggage somewhere on the boat, so I was grateful to have a cabin to myself. I imagined the Recliner Lounge full of fidgety and snoring passengers, and again said "thank you" to whatever's watching over me.

Generally I am a very heavy sleeper and don't wake during the night except to pee. But this night I woke up several times to the rolling motion of the ferry. My stomach was a bit queasy, but each time I took a moment to look out into the night. From the window, I could look down on the immense rolling waves that were strangely lit up by some light above me. The southern sky was full of stars. I felt such a stillness and awe looking out that window. If journeys are preceded by an initiation, this voyage was that for me. I was in some unfathomable way connecting with this Bass Strait, and preparing for the journey ahead. And unknowingly, I was connecting with so much more.

When my alarm jarred me awake, I jumped up and peered out the window at a bright sunny morning. In the distance I could see land. Tasmania at last!

I took the fastest shower on record, and was so happy I didn't have to share this small space with three others. Unfortunately my clean clothes were also in my checked baggage, but I was too excited to care. I gathered my things and dashed upstairs.

From the railing I could see the sun shining on the beautiful green coastline. The air felt so brisk and fresh, the cleanest air in the world, apparently. There was a strange square looking mountain off to the west. "That's the Nut," offered one of the locals who saw me staring.

Docking the ferry and disembarking happened so quickly I missed it. After collecting my bags and clearing the sniffer dog, I walked out of the terminal building wondering what happens next. How do I cross the river to get to the town? Where do I go to stumble upon a ride to Smithton? I could have asked one of these departing passengers if they were going that way, but they were already gone.

My First Day in Tassie

I was walking slowly towards the terminal building when suddenly it just dawned on me. It wasn't really a thought, but I *knew* I could drive here without a problem. Perfect! That solved all my problems. I would get the car for two days to go to Smithton and back. After that I could take the bus down through western Tassie where all the logging trucks were. Brilliant idea! Why hadn't I thought of that! And Hertz was having a special! (My cheap side was happy too.)

I found my car in the parking lot and put my luggage in the trunk. Looking around to get my bearings, I realized there is no traffic — not another car anywhere. I can't imagine how all those vehicles got off the ferry and disappeared so quickly, but I'm grateful they did. Then I remembered it's 7:30 Sunday morning and most of Tassie was still asleep.

That has to be in my favor. I wouldn't want to attempt this with traffic.

I walked up to the passenger side of the car to get in — the first of many such mistakes. Sheepishly, I hurried around to the driver's side, hoping no one noticed. At least the ignition was in the same place. Fortunately it was an automatic transmission, I didn't think I could have handled left-handed shifting today. I started the car and found my way to the exit. I put on my right blinker and suddenly the windshield wipers were wiping away.

"Oops! They're reversed here. If that's the worst mistake I make, I'll be just fine."

Maybe it's like riding a bike. I thought as I pulled out onto the road and found my way to the main highway. *Just remember to keep yourself along the center line — a mirror image of what you're used to*, I reminded myself, thinking back to my left-handed driving experiences a few years ago.

I crossed over the river and headed into Devonport, arriving at the tourist office parking lot. I felt quite accomplished to have stayed on the left side of the road so far. I also thanked the heavens that it's Sunday morning.

The tourist office was open only for the ferry arrival, and obviously all the other passengers had either moved on or didn't stop. I quickly glanced through the brochures for anything of interest.

"Can I help you find something?" asked one of the staff. She and her co-worker were the only people in the place.

"Can you give me directions to Tiagarra? I was hoping to go see the Aboriginal Cultural Center Museum the guide book raved about."

"Well, it's just down this road, but it's closed on Sundays. Will you be around tomorrow?"

"Oh!" I groaned in disappointment, "I really wanted to see that. No, I'm heading over to Smithton today. But maybe I can stop in when I return the car."

"There is a nice walk along the bluff where there are some indigenous rock engravings. That's always open," she offered.

I considered this possibility, but wasn't feeling moved to go on a bluff walk. It would be better to just get on the road before everyone wakes up and makes driving more challenging. (Later I realized that all of northern Tassie is pretty rural, and on Sunday just about everyone stays home — all day.)

"Could you tell me where I can get some groceries?" I would definitely need some provisions for the drive.

"I'm sorry, all the stores are closed on Sunday." Seeing my disappointment she added," If you're driving west, you could stop in Burnie. There's a big Coles there that will be open."

"Okay, great, thanks," I waved, and headed out the door.

I circled the car until I found the driver's door, and wiped my windshield again before I pulled out onto the correct side of the street.

I'm getting the hang of this, I thought. *If I can just remember which side has the driver's door.*

Back on the highway, I relaxed into driving and started to notice the scenery. It was a very "civilized" countryside, with neat little houses and fields. Yet, I could feel the clear, crisp wildness of Tassie underneath this "foreign overlay" of British colonization. Somehow the coming of the white man had not really touched the deep essence of this land — it was still itself. I was actually quite surprised to be able to feel it so strongly, especially in an area that was covered in farms instead of bush. I drove along just feeling into the land and being so grateful to be here.

I had been reading my Tassie travel guide for two months now, trying to learn what I could about the place, but more importantly to get a feel for where I was being called. I had picked out a few possibilities, yet now that I was here I discovered I didn't really feel a pull. I decided to trust that. I knew this journey was not just about having fun, but seemed to have some sort of purpose that was yet unknown to me. I was tempted when I saw the sign for the town of Penguin, a place with a fairy penguin rookery. Yet even that felt like too much trouble.

By the time I reached Burnie it was 10 am, so I could call Hart — about 8 pm her time. I was comfortable enough driving to feel okay about entering a bigger town and navigating the streets. I just had to remember how to turn a corner and end up in the correct lane — especially on the multiple-lane streets.

Keep yourself next to the center line, I kept reminding myself.

After getting some groceries in Cole's, I found a quiet place to park and give the cell phone a try.

"Hello, Hart, I'm in Tassie!"

"Great, Sue. How was the trip?"

I told her about the ferry ride and my good fortune with the cabin angel. I also told her what I had sensed about the crisp wildness of the land and the palpable overlay of colonization.

"Sue, there's some sort of energy next to your left elbow. Are you aware of it?"

"No, not really. Can you tell what it is?" I was so used to not feeling the things that people would see and feel around me. Yet it happened so often, I just enjoyed being clued in for a change.

"It feels like some sort of group energy. Not individuals, but like an Aboriginal group consciousness. I think they joined you on the ferry crossing," she offered.

So finally I learned who I had had an 'appointment' to meet on the crossing. I suspected riding on the water was some sort of initiation into this whole adventure.

"They want to show you some things, and then they'll go with you to Hunter Island. You need to go some places first," she added.

"Hmmm. I wonder where. Let me get my map. I'm heading to Smithton to hopefully meet the boat guy. Is it on the way there?"

"Tell me the names of the towns on the way there," Hart asked.

"How about Rocky Cape National Park. There are some Aboriginal caves there that I can walk to." This was one of those areas that had attracted me.

"No . . . where else?"

"Wynyard, Boat Harbor, Sisters Beach, Rocky Cape, Port Latta . . ."

"That's it, Port Latta. What's there?" Hart wondered.

"I don't know. The guidebook doesn't say anything about it, it's just on the map."

"Well, Sue, they want you to go walk on the beach there for some reason. But there's also someplace else."

"All right, next is Black River, then Stanley? There's something called The Nut in Stanley," I said as I remembered the gigantic formation I had seen from the ferry.

"No, that's not it. What else is there, Sue?"

"Well, the next town is Smithton. But there are some things beyond Smithton. There's Woolnorth . . ." I said as I adjusted the map.

"Are there any other places with Aboriginal sites?" she wondered.

"Out on the west coast is a place called Marrawah, or Preminghana. It's land that's been returned to the indigenous people. I'm not sure whether it's possible to visit there or not. I read you need a guide to go there."

"Well, that's where they want you to go. Those two places. I don't know why, but it's important for you to go to these places before your trip to Hunter Island. It's like they're trying to prepare you somehow. By the way, how does getting to the island look," Hart inquired.

"I called the guy yesterday before I left Melbourne and he said that the wind was still really strong and he thought the water would be too rough. So I asked if I could just check back in tonight to see if anything has changed."

"It still feels like a go," she said quietly.

"I think so, too. But I got an interesting email from one of my friends. She's very concerned about me going to Hunter Island. She feels I'm in danger and don't need to go there physically to do what I'm meant to do."

"I don't see that Sue, but how do you feel about it?"

"For several weeks now I have been seeing massive waves — the kind that tower above a boat. I can feel the intense motion, and the fear and even sinking to the bottom of the sea. This is unusual for me, and I suspect I may have drowned here in another lifetime," I explained.

"Yeah, that feels true," Hart offered.

"But I'm still feeling very strongly to go, even if I end up drowning in big waves." I was surprised to hear myself say that, but I could feel the deep certainty that was pulling me. Maybe it was the portal's tractor beam or the call of destiny, but it felt so important that I go through with this. I could feel that the wave of energy that was carrying me was heading straight for Hunter Island, and there was nothing in me that wanted to resist.

"Well, I don't think that's what happens," she laughed. "Let me know how it all goes."

After we hung up I sat there in the sunshine. I felt so elated to be in this time and space. At last I was in Tasmania. It was like a dream, yet crystal-clear reality. I had no idea what to expect except the little insights offered by my psychic friends and the astrologers. And of course those subtle glimmers of knowing that occurred within me. I knew it would be life-changing — I had been feeling that since before the three weeks that started it all. I also knew the experience could be understated, as most things are for me. I was hoping for something more concrete this time. After all, I had basically jumped off the cliff into this experience. Wouldn't it be nice to have something obvious as a result? Then I wouldn't feel like I sound nuts.

Oh well, time will tell, I think to myself. *I will be happy with however this turns out. It feels so right and important to me, even if no one else understands.*

Port Latta

The roads in Tassie were fairly narrow with no shoulders. I can't imagine what people do when their car breaks down or they get a flat tire. Yet, they were wide enough for my little rental car to lean way left when the big trucks came whizzing by.

I had been watching the map, so I knew when I was getting close to Port Latta. Even so, I was surprised to see the sign in the middle of nowhere. I was expecting to see a few houses or a little town. I turned the car around and followed the sign into the road indicated, and sat there with my mouth hanging open.

In front of me, on the edge of the sea, was a huge building that looked like a run-down old warehouse or factory of some kind. There were a few cars in the parking lot, but nothing else. There was a big granite monument to explain what was going on here. Apparently iron ore from within Tassie is slurried here through a pipeline, processed, and then loaded onto ships. That explained the two-kilometer pier out into the water.

I parked and walked to the edge of the lot to look down at the beach. It was a very steep embankment with no way to get down. I remembered Hart had said they wanted me to walk on the beach, and now I was just confused.

I went inside the building looking for a clue as to why I was here or maybe get directions to some beach access. It was just an empty office, obviously meant for the employees. I waited a few minutes but there were no signs of life, so I left.

I walked along the parking lot to see if the embankment would yield access anywhere, but eventually gave up. Not knowing what else to do, I finally got in my car and headed down the road again. About a kilometer farther I saw another road and instinctively turned in. It was a little dirt road with a few houses on it to the left. I headed right which took me toward the beach and a place to park, then headed back toward Port Latta.

I started listening intently inside for any sense of why I was here, what I was to do, or what "they" wanted me to know. As I walked I marveled at the amount of stuff I had to step over. I've never really been a shell collector, even though as a kid we went to the beach every summer. Any beach I'd ever seen was mostly empty with an occasional something washing up. This beach was full of all sorts of shells, sponges, seaweed, driftwood and trash.

After the first stretch of sand, I came to a section of rocks where really interesting shells had washed up. They were so beautiful and like none I had seen before. I picked some up with the idea to bring them to friends in the US. After I had chosen a handful of the best ones, I looked farther along and saw there were actually zillions. Suddenly faced with so many, they lost their appeal. Obviously they were something common and not worth collecting. And besides, my hands were freezing.

I started to ponder the nature of value. It seemed so stupid that the quantity available affected their value, but isn't that the law of supply and demand? The Universe seems to be such an amazingly abundant place, why would something be less valued just because they were numerous? I was caught between my logic and my deep knowing, so just dropped it along with the shells. I realized that I don't collect shells anyway, why would I start today?

Around the bend, I could see that big rectangle of an ugly processing plant rising from the land. Behind it were some slurry piles, and then the long, long pier out into the sea. This was a very dismal place.

So why am I here? What is it you want me to see? After feeling nothing for fifteen minutes, I decide it's a mystery and I might as well continue my drive.

Walking back, as I crossed the rocks, I noticed the interesting patterns. I love patterns wherever they occur, and I had never seen rocks like this before. The rocks were "cut" in rectangular shapes the size of a loaf pan. In between these rectangles was what looked like metal icing oozing out. It stuck out a couple of inches and then started to curl. Obviously this ore 'icing' was stronger than the surrounding rock and less susceptible to erosion. I just kept staring at it, never having seen naturally occurring metal before. I wondered what made it look like metal instead of rock. But rocks don't curl, and it had the look of crude iron. I guess that's what they're processing in that plant.

I took a couple of photos and headed back to the car, wondering why "they" wanted me to stop here. Some questions take longer than others to be answered, and this one took six months. It was in the middle of a conversation with a friend from Mystery School. When I told her about reading Robert Lawlor's book she remembered hearing an interview with him on internet radio. The thing that most stood out for her in the program was when he talked about the aborigines being telepathic. One had recently told him that they were losing this gift because the metal was being mined from the planet. In that moment I *knew* this was the answer to my question — something they wanted me to know — another of the puzzle pieces to keep with me for some future connection.

Marrawah and Preminghana

The next stop was a few hours away. The big trucks passed frequently, always causing the car to swerve. With every one, I held my breath and gripped the wheel tightly. Overall I was comfortable driving now. I still turned on my wipers to signal, but I got over that eventually.

As I drove toward Stanley, I could see the Nut rising from the sea. It was impressive from the ferry, but now it looked humongous — rising straight out of the sea, with a totally flat top. The town nestled at its base was completely dwarfed. I was tempted to turn in and take a closer look, but I've never been a great sightseer. I'm always more interested in the feel of a place, its people and customs rather than its tourist attractions. Yet I love to see what unusual delights nature has created. On the way back, perhaps.

As I continued to drive west I considered again that this may be a very subtle journey for me. My psychic and intuitive friends can see so much more of what happens on the other levels than I can. I would most likely be unaware if they didn't tell me. Yet I have inklings and hunches and whims and thoughts. And when they tell me what they see and sense, it's amazing how often I've actually been picking up on these same things.

I was hoping on this adventure, that had so dramatically pulled me out of my life, that my experiences would be more noticeable to me. I could feel that if things stay subtle it will make me a little sad, but I'm willing to follow this through even if whatever is meant to happen is all below my radar. Feeling such a sense of rightness will just have to suffice and carry me through. It seems to be the best barometer I have to tell if I'm on the right track.

Until now, the drive had been along the coast, very picturesque and notably rural. Passing the signs to Smithton, I began to veer southwest and away from the coast. That's when I realized that what had seemed rural was actually quite populated by comparison to where I was headed. The road was still paved, but suddenly there was no traffic — not a single car or truck. There were no intersecting roads or houses for miles — and miles — not even a driveway or side road.

The only sign the entire way was for Dismal Swamp, where I could slide 110 meters down into a Blackwood sinkhole. I smiled, remembering the guidebook's description . . . "The view from inside the toilet cubicles across the tree top canopy is superb." Hmmm — tempting, but I decide to leave the inspiring toilet vista for another time.

I was expecting Marrawah to be a little town, so was surprised to find only a tiny general store and a few houses. I grabbed some tea and read what the Lonely Planet guidebook had to say about the area . . .

> *The Marrawah area, with its isolated west-coast beaches and cliffs, has seen minimal disturbance from European development, in direct contrast to the maximal disturbances visited by Europeans upon the area's former Aboriginal inhabitants – these include the massacre of an estimated 30 Aborigines in 1827 at the aptly named Cape Grim to the north, apparently in response to the slaughter of a flock of sheep. Particular areas have now been proclaimed reserves to protect the relics, including rock carvings, middens, and hut depressions . . . But arguably the most important Aboriginal art site in the area, if not the state, can be found seven km north of Marrawah at Preminghana – drive along the gravel road north of the Marrawah General Store and take the first turn left.*

So I did as told — and found the turn with no problem. I followed the dirt track in, not knowing whether I could actually visit without having arranged a tour with a guide as the book instructs. Eventually I came to a little car park with some instructions. I was allowed to be here, and I could follow the track to the beach, but that's all that's open to the public. I can't go see the rock carvings, middens, or hut depressions.

Hmmm. Maybe I don't need to see those things, I think to myself and head off.

There was an easy sandy track through the scrub to a beautiful wide white beach with very little debris except for cuttlefish shells.

My best guess was to turn left, but I could just have easily turned right. When I was a kid we played "pin the tail on the donkey" at birthday parties. They would blindfold you and spin you around and then point you in a direction and say "go." Then you'd stumble forward until you ran into something and then you'd stick the donkey tail you've been carrying onto the wall or chair or whatever you've run into. It felt a lot like that, except I wasn't carrying a tail, and there wasn't any audible squealing to signal if I was getting closer. (That doesn't mean there wasn't laughing involved somewhere.)

As I walked along, I found myself thinking about the infinity symbol. I stopped and drew one in the sand — upright like an eight, along with 'YES.' Remembering how I had used the symbol to connect my head and heart while talking with Hart, I took a step to the right so the sand symbol was now connecting my shadow's head and heart. Then it occurred to me to hold the gyrating infinity symbol in the center of my head again as Hart had instructed.

Hmmm. That feels really good.

Then, without thinking, I put the gyrating infinity symbol in my heart chakra, then my root chakra, then at my feet and also deep into the earth and above my head. All six symbols were rapidly gyrating simultaneously. It felt great, but I really didn't know why I did that.

Then I turned and began heading back up the beach, as if in response to an unspoken instruction, "Okay, you're done here." Yet I hadn't heard anything but the sea.

This had happened to me a few times before, where I found myself responding to something that I hadn't heard with either my outer or inner ear. I responded as if I had heard it, by answering or doing as directed. Often it's when I notice myself responding that I realize that there's been some sort of communication with . . . whatever.

Once, while driving in a very rural area in New Hampshire, I found myself turning into a hardware store in the middle of nowhere. I was quite surprised because I knew of no reason to go to a hardware store. I heard myself mutter "OK," and entered the store. I wandered up and down the aisles asking silently, *All right, what is it? What's in here that you want me to see?* When I finally found it, *I knew it.* There at the end of an aisle were some beautiful leather boots — something I had been wanting — lace-up, lined, black, soft leather, half price. And out of three pairs, they had my size. I was stunned, grateful, and walked out with the boots. I would never have found such perfect boots if I had been looking for them, and I would never have thought to look for them there.

I've also noticed, ever since the event in Albuquerque, that as I have grown to trust and follow that silent voice, it's been happening more often. And usually it results in a wonderful blessing of some kind. So, I don't tend to worry myself over who or what it is I'm hearing silently. Whoever it is obviously cares for me and is helping me in ways both big and small.

The walk back to the car was short and uneventful. It's quite noticeable to me when I'm finished somewhere. Suddenly there's absolutely no energy or interest, and I'm just ready to move on.

My map showed only one road heading north from Marrawah, and that is all there is. "Guess I won't be getting lost," I smiled. I'd been in Tassie almost twelve hours now and covered a lot of ground but had barely talked to anyone other than Hart.

***

It was time to call the fisherman to see about tomorrow, and as I neared Smithton my phone finally beeped with service. I pulled over and gave Terry a ring.

"Yeah?" A man's gruff voice answered.

"Hi, Terry, this is Sue. I'm in Smithton now and wondering if it looks like we can go to Hunter Island tomorrow." I hear a groan on the other end of the line.

"I don't know, Sue. The wind is still really strong and I'm not sure it would be safe. But the weather is supposed to change soon. We should be able to make the trip on Tuesday." Now it's my turn to groan. Every time Hart and I have looked at this, she is quite certain that this galactic portal will only be open on October 8 — tomorrow.

"I can't go on Tuesday," I said with a bit of a whine. Then I mumbled something about needing to keep moving to get my rental car back on time or something lame like that. I didn't think telling him I was trying to keep a date with a galactic portal would help my case much. It sounded insane to me, and I'm me.

"Is it okay if I call you in the morning to see if anything has changed?" I practically pleaded. All I knew to do was to keep trying for a different outcome in another moment.

"I'll check the weather in the morning and then I'll give you a call. It'll be about 6 am. Would that be all right?" Terry asked without much enthusiasm.

"Yes, Terry, that would be great. I'll talk to you then. Goodbye." I was thrilled — it wasn't a yes, but my hopes weren't dashed yet.

I was mulling over this news when I arrived in Smithton and decided to proceed as if I would be going in the morning. First I checked into the only hotel in town. It was old and tired, with high ceilings and threadbare bedspreads. At first they gave me a room with a door I couldn't lock, and a window onto the hallway that also didn't lock. Looking back, I would have been perfectly safe, but I was used to being cautious. The new room was just as tired, but from the window I could see the boat ramp we'd be using — if we go.

I don't even know why I need to go there. Am I nuts? I decided possibly, but I headed toward the only ATM in town to withdraw the cash. I'd been stressing some about the cost of this strange adventure. It seemed like a lot to spend for just two hours with a galactic portal. Before I pushed the amount needed, I asked one more time, "If I spend $500 on this portal rendezvous, will I still have what I need to finish the rest of my trip?" And once again I got a yes.

Chapter 15

Date with Destiny

Usually I'm a really heavy sleeper, and need multiple alarms to wake up. And as I struggle between sleep and full consciousness, things surface in my mind — feelings, ideas, knowing.

But that night in Smithton, I slept soundly and woke up before my alarm, even though it was only 5:30. And when I woke up I wasn't aware of anything — not a thought in my head. I sat up, looked around, feeling foggy and confused. I knew something exciting and important was happening this day, but it took me a moment to remember what.

And then it slowly dawned on me — I had finally reached the day — October 8. Soon I would know whether this was happening.

"I have a date with a galactic portal," I mumbled and then smiled, realizing I had no apprehensions about it.

Not since the tractor beam got hold of me in Colin's Toilet, I thought silently, and then laughed remembering that conversation.

I jumped out of bed and hurried around getting dressed and having a bit of brekky. *You're in Oz now, you might as well call it brekky!* I smiled at the thought.

I was ready to go so quickly, and then just sat on the bed waiting for the call. Tic, tic, tic. There wasn't a ticking clock nearby, but there might as well have been. After waiting forever, I decided to ring Terry.

"Morning, Terry, this is Sue. I was just wondering how things look this morning," I asked with a prayer in my heart.

"G'day, Sue. I was just going to call you. Might be too windy today, but tomorrow looks good." He said cheerily.

"But I can't go tomorrow, I have to be somewhere," I said slowly. "I'm so disappointed." The disappointment was true, the appointment was a slight fib. My appointment was today with the portal on Hunter.

After a bit of a pause, Terry piped up. "Do you get seasick easily? If we go today, it could be quite rough. I don't like to take people out when it's going to be choppy."

"I'll be honest Terry, I have gotten nauseous on occasion, but I don't whinge! (Aussie slang for whine.) I promise not to complain, and not to barf on your boat," I offered, hoping I could keep my promise.

"Okay, Sue, we'll go today. Meet me at the boat ramp across from the Bridge Hotel in an hour," he said with a hint of resignation.

"Great Terry. Thanks. I'll see you there," I replied, trying not to squeal. I was beside myself with gratitude and excitement.

An hour, what am I going to do with an hour, I thought. *Better call Hart and let her know it's a go.*

"Thank you to whoever has made this possible," I whispered to everyone, as I dialed the phone.

"Hi, Hart. The fisherman has agreed to take me," I almost shrieked into the phone. "He told me to wait till tomorrow, but I told him I couldn't. Finally he agreed."

"That's great, Sue. I can't wait to find out what happens there," Hart replied.

"It will probably be as subtle as every other adventure I go on," I said with a bit of sadness. I already knew not to expect to be aware of much of anything, but to enjoy myself anyway.

Hart was quiet for a moment, then asked, "Sue, do you feel anything around your head? I think it's more of that group Aboriginal consciousness I mentioned yesterday. Can you feel them?"

"No, but what else is new?" I scoffed. "But I did wake up a bit strange today. I woke before the alarm, and I couldn't remember what was happening today. I just knew it was important or exciting or something."

"Yeah, they are the same ones that joined you coming across the strait. They cloaked you during the night and are helping prepare you for Hunter Island." Hart said matter-of-factly.

"Well good. I need all the help I can get. I better go now, just wanted to let you know the good news. So if I don't drown, I'll let you know how it goes." We both laughed.

"I don't think you'll be drowning today, Sue. I just can't feel it anywhere."

Wild Ride to Hunter

I arrived at the boat dock quite early. I didn't care, I was just too excited to wait. I looked back at my hotel, and there was a rainbow coming out of the room where I had stayed. And on the river were some pelicans. I had seen some in Cairns too, so I took both as a great sign.

When Terry showed up, I was surprised that he had just a normal speed boat, like you'd water ski behind. And then I noticed the name: **Comfort Zone**.

How perfect is that? I expected this trip would be out of my comfort zone, but apparently not. I smiled at the thought.

As we headed out into Duck Bay, Terry got on his cell and called someone. I heard him ask if they would be able to be picked up today. He would be in the area soon, and would need to pick them up in about three hours. Would that work for them?

I knew he was calling Jane on Three Hummock. I had talked with her briefly last evening, and knew he was picking them up tomorrow for a supply run.

"We'll have a full boat on the way back," he shouted to me over the noise of the engine. "I'll go pick up the folks on Three Hummock after I drop you on Hunter's. I was gonna get them tomorrow, but they're willing to come today."

Ah, so that's why he wanted me to wait until tomorrow. I thought. *Thank you again, whoever nudged him into today!* I chuckled as I pictured angels whispering in his ear to say yes to me. He really had no reason to do it, so I figured someone was encouraging him.

The engine was loud, so it wasn't really easy to talk. But he filled me in on the islands we were going to be skirting. It was obvious you needed to know what you were doing to navigate these waters.

"It doesn't seem too windy," I said naively. "Maybe we got lucky."

"Just wait till we get out of Duck Bay and into open waters," he chuckled. "And the wind always picks up as the day gets on. It'll be a real ride when we're coming back." He laughed again, but didn't seem worried or nervous, so neither was I.

I had learned long ago how to use the acupressure points on my wrists to keep me from barfing. Hopefully they were up to today's challenge.

"So where on Hunter Island do you want me to take you?" he asked.

"I don't know exactly," I answered honestly.

"Well, I could drop you at Cave Bay easy enough," he offered.

"Is that where the Aboriginal cave is?" I replied hopefully.

"Yeah, it's there. You may not be able to get to it with the tide high. But you'll be able to see it when we are heading in."

"Sounds great!" I had known there was a cave there with a midden dating back 12,000 years. It didn't even occur to me to try and see it.

"Did you manage to get hold of the leaseholder?" Terry swerved to avoid submerged rocks as he asked this. "Whoa! They come up quick! I'm glad I know these waters!"

"Me too," I giggled nervously. "Yeah, I did call him. He was pretty nice the first time I called, telling me about the flooded landing strip and the feral cows. But when I called him back saying I could get a ride with you, he wasn't so nice. I think my persistence annoyed him." Terry nodded knowingly.

"He did say that his leasehold only went to the high water mark," I continued, "so he couldn't stop me from going to the beach. I assured him that I would respect his leasehold and not go inland at all."

"So why are you going to this island anyway?" Terry looked over as he asked this question. He hadn't asked me this before now, which surprised me. I couldn't wait to hear what would come out of my mouth. I paused and took a deep breath . . . .

Why was I going to this island anyway? Should I tell him about spirits calling me? Or that my psychic friend said I had to start here? Or maybe that there's a galactic portal opening for me today? I smiled as I thought of all these possible answers.

"It's a bit hard to explain, and I don't really expect you to understand. I'm not even sure I understand, but I have one of those unexplainable urges — a calling, you might say — to come here and be here for a moment. When I have these urges and follow them, amazing things happen in my life. When I ignore these urges, life sort of sucks." I was watching the water as I shared.

"Fair enough," he said with his eyes on the water.

We were silent for a long time after that.

I thought about Jackie's warning only once during the ride, only to notice that I felt safe and right and guided. I was exhilarated that I was almost there — about to experience an unknown moment that I couldn't possibly prepare for or anticipate.

"There's Hunter there," he pointed. "And you can see the cave. It's that dark spot in the rocks to the right of the beach. Oh, look — there's a pair of sea eagles there. See them circling? That's rare to see them — there's only a few pairs left."

It was obvious he was happy about this so it must be a good sign. As we got closer, he swung around in front of the cave so I could get a better look and take some pictures. I could tell by the water level and the rocks that this was going to be as close as I'd get.

He idled up as close to the beach as he was able to safely. "Here are my old waders. If you put them on, you can slip over the side into the shallow water and walk to the beach." He handed me a very heavy rubber contraption and chuckled as I tried to figure it out.

Looking fashionable on my way to meet a portal.

Once they were on, I collected my backpack and proceeded to slide off the side of the boat. It was quite a strange feeling, the water pushing the rubber waders up against my legs. Fortunately, it was only three feet deep with no waves.

"Now just be careful walking in those. You don't want to fall over!" He laughed loudly. "That would be a real catastrophe."

I grinned at the visual, and walked with great care.

"I'll go over to Three Hummock and have a cuppa. I'll be back in about two hours or so." He had already started turning the boat around.

"You right?" he yelled, looking back.

I gave him a thumbs-up and he was off.

I had assumed he would be sitting in the bay waiting for me while I had my appointment with destiny, so I felt quite lucky that he had somewhere to go and I was here alone.

I slowly waded through the water, chuckling again about the thought of falling and the waders filling with water.

Oh, my gosh, Sue, that would be the klutziest move ever, you'd have to swim out of the waders to save yourself.

The Portal is Open

When I finally sat on the white sand beach to take off the waders I let out a big sigh. I was finally here. I closed my eyes and just felt. I wasn't one to feel energies or things other people felt, but I could feel the silence, the grace. I especially loved places where you couldn't hear a single man-made noise.

I started to explore a bit. There was an old shed on one end of the beach and some rusty iron rails going into the water. That must be how the leaseholder was able to drop off his feral cows and pick them up later.

I climbed up the rocky outcropping and tried to pick my way around it to see if it was possible to get closer to the cave. But as Terry had predicted, the tide was so high I would have to mountain-goat my way around, and I knew that wasn't happening.

So I went back to the beach and started to walk, looking for shells as I went.

Yeah, I just paid $500 to collect shells from Hunter Island. I snickered quietly as I thought of the absurdity of my life sometimes.

"All right, you guys. You brought me here for something. What's up," I mumbled to "them," trying to figure out what to do now that I was here. I considered a few possibilities, but opted for the gyrating infinity symbol, discovering that four points were added above my head. Suddenly I felt clear, and felt that I just needed to sink back into the timelessness of the waves and sky.

Silence.

It was a beautiful silence. Gentle waves lapped at the shore. Sea birds squawked and the wind blew softly. The sun mostly shining except for a quick sprinkling or two. I continued to walk, collect shells and ponder why I was here. As was normal for me, I couldn't feel anything to tell about. No signs of a portal or Aboriginal spirits or anything.

I tried not to be disappointed and just stay in the moment. This had happened to me so many times before, and later my psychic friends would fill me in on what had transpired. They were always telling me that this time I would feel something, but so far I was still a rock. But by now I knew quite deeply, that I was just wired differently. And I didn't know for what. But I was called to be here, so here I was, just being.

As I walked the beach I came to a little rivulet flowing out of the bush. It zigzagged like a snake, cutting into the soft beach sand. Filled with the tannins of eucalyptus, the water was shades of brown. I squatted to watch. As the sun shone through the little ripples, the patterns of light danced along the bottom of the water. It was electrifying — all the shooting patterns, the glimmers, the flashes of light. Absolutely mesmerizing. I tried to catch it on film, but it's difficult to catch something that's so alive.

I stood, moved up the rivulet, and had a thought, *Okay guys, I need a sign to let me know things are as they should be.* Immediately, a large chunk of sand fell into the water.

"That was quick. Thanks," I was a good foot away from the bank and hadn't moved, so I was happy to take that as my sign. Not much information in it, however.

"I wonder if that means the portal is open," I whispered. Then I had a thoughtless thought and opened my purse looking for the strange piece of shell I had picked up on Coolum Beach last week.

It was the top of a small conch-type shell, but all that was left was a circular fragment. The outside was worn smooth, but on the inside you could still see the spiraling ridges left from its chambers. And in the very middle was a hole that was blocked — wedged with sand. I had tried to dislodge it by blowing or banging it on a rock, but it wouldn't budge. I liked the spiral pattern and I felt compelled to keep it. Even this morning I'd seen it in my purse with the hole still blocked.

So when I pulled the shell out now, the hole was clear. I was stunned — I *knew* the portal was open. I closed my eyes and felt into the moment.

The portal is open.

So why does such a momentous moment feel so ordinary? I wondered. I was sure that my friends would feel lots of things here, but maybe feeling wasn't what mattered.

Many times, my friends had suggested that perhaps I was being activated, or activating as I wandered on my travels. Maybe I was being downloaded or acting as an acupuncture point on the earth. All nice ideas, and maybe true.

I may never know why I'm called to such strange places to feel nothing, I thought, chuckling, as I wandered back up the beach.

But what I do get, whenever I follow these urges and this thoughtless guidance, is a deep, deep sense of rightness. Of feeling like I'm right where I'm meant to be, to do what I'm meant to do, even if my little human ego doesn't get to know what it is.

With that thought, I suspected I'd done everything I could do and I was just sitting on the sand wondering how soon they'd pick me up. I thought about Hart's husband, Michael, and the fact that he's been looking at things metaphysically lately and that's how he saw the blue line and the acupuncture points in the field.

I don't think I've ever looked at things metaphysically, I thought. *I should try it now with Hunter Island. Maybe the galactic portal will help.* I looked around to the right and the beach looked normal.

Ok, nothing noteworthy, I thought and was about to give up.

Wait, not so fast. Keep looking, I encouraged myself.

I turned to the left and looked at the hillside, and gasped. Every single leaf on every tree was twinkling at me.

It's just rained, and I'm sure the wind is blowing the leaves, my mind chimed in, but I ignored it and kept looking.

The entire hillside was glittering, even the rocks. Sparkling like sun on the sea, like nothing I'd ever seen. It took my breath away. I couldn't believe how the entire hillside was blessing me and celebrating — glistening with life.

I tried to take a picture of that as well, knowing it would never do it justice.

I suddenly felt moved and wandered into an area of rocks covered with orange and yellow lichen, and with sparse vegetation in between. As soon as I entered this area, this circle, I felt it — a deep sacredness. A deep, deep silence — and presence. *Their* presence.

This all comes without thought, just an instant recognition and knowing. They were here waiting for me. So I sat on a rock and closed my eyes and sank into the deep silence with them. I felt welcome, safe, and I knew why I was here.

After an eternity of silence, I began talking silently to them . . . .

I want to honor you all, for being what you are. You were designed to keep everything as it was on the first day. And you have done that perfectly for longer than we even know.

My people, the white European tribe, are not designed that way. And because of that, we did not recognize or appreciate your beauty, your gifts, or your perfection. Much suffering was caused to you because of this. Our design is neither better nor worse, just different.

I am here to heal my tribe and to try to understand why we've been so aggressive and destructive to the earth and all life on it.

I pause and feel until I know where to go next. I launched into the Ho'oponopono that I learned in Mystery School . . . .

If I or my ancestors have ever hurt, injured or caused you or your ancestors to suffer, I am deeply, deeply sorry. Please forgive me, I love you. Thank you.

That felt good, but then I got a better idea — something that would clear things up for both tribes.

I would like to connect to all of you on a soul level.

I'd like to connect to all of my ancestors who have been involved.

And recognize the agreements that we have made in spirit and honored in form. All the agreements to hurt each other, cause each other to suffer, regardless of who does the harm or who is harmed.

We are able to break these agreements in their entirety, past, present, and future, so the effects can leave us all, and the karma can be unraveled for all. And I invite each of you to do so, whichever tribe you belong to. You may accept this invitation and break these agreements now. Or the invitation will remain outside of time and space for eternity until you are ready. To accept it, all you need to do is to hope for a better life, desire to be happy, or wish to be free.

I could feel the rush of energy, rightness. I was filled with a sweet euphoria of freedom and release. This went so far beyond forgiveness — to a place before the occurrence. To a place where both sides are free of the effects and of the karma. To a place where it's recognized and understood that we have made some really bad agreements from ignorance or not understanding.

But we need not carry this baggage, these wounds, this karma, any longer.

I disconnected from their souls and sat for a while, feeling the rightness, the joy, the completeness. It felt so celebratory in such a sweet, quiet way. I felt a gentle sprinkle of rain and opened my eyes to see the hillside twinkling at me again.

About this time I heard the **Comfort Zone** buzzing across the water. I struggled back into the hip waders, then turned to the island, to the portal, to the Aboriginal spirits, and expressed my delight and gratitude for such a glorious day.

Mission Accomplished!

**

There was only time for quick introductions with Jane and her family while Terry turned the boat around.

"The wind has picked up. It's going to be a whole lot rougher going back. Hang on, guys." He yelled as he took off.

He wasn't kidding. The wind was gusting and the waves were massive. As each one hit the boat, we were splashed with water — by the bucketful — deluged with each cresting wave. Over and over. Several times he had to swerve quickly, and I was sure someone was going overboard.

It was a long, bumpy, wet ride back, but I had such joy in my heart. I knew something monumental had just happened, and I had done what I had come for.

I didn't really understand fully what I had done, and maybe never would. But when I called Hart on the road later that day, she shared some interesting things.

"Sue, you have a sort of yellow disk around your head, kind of like the rings of Saturn. And I can feel the Aboriginal group consciousness is very grateful for your honoring of them, for your recognizing them in wholeness, and recognizing the wrongs committed against them. And they are very grateful to have these agreements broken — to be free." Hart paused before continuing.

"And something else has happened. Remember that metaphysical level that Michael and I stumbled on recently. Well, suddenly there are lots more lights there, more souls popping up. And you've popped up to that level, too."

"That's fantastic Hart. It will be interesting to see if I feel any different." I smiled and knew not to get my hopes up.

I was forever grateful to Hart for filling in some of the information and energetic things for me, otherwise I would continue to think I was a rock and feel like nothing was going on. I am quite certain I would have never made it this far without her direction and insight. And yet the experience of this day was not subtle for me. It was pristine.

I was parked by the sea, and was pondering the day. *So, Sue, what does a galactic portal feel like?*

I paused and really felt deeply into my being. Finally, I listened to the words coming out of my mouth . . . "It feels like pristine clarity."

I realized the whole visit to Hunter Island was so precious and deeply etched with such pristine clarity — in my memory, in my psyche, in my body and in my being.

I immediately fell into a deep, deep sleep.

Chapter 16

Moving Through Tassie

My next official appointment — with primal terror — was five days away, so I thought I was just doing what visitors do in Tasmania. I had stopped in Strahan with plans to take the Gordon River Cruise.

It was nice enough, a trip around Macquarie Harbour to pass through Hell's Gate, the narrow entrance to the harbor that opens up to the Southern Ocean. I was particularly interested in the ingenuity used to build sea walls under the water to keep this channel open, and made a mental note to share the pictures with my engineer dad.

The tour also went to Sarah Island, my first convict station, home to some of the "criminals" that were transported from England. It was the beginning of a deepening sense of the despair and hopelessness the convicts suffered.

But then we were dropped off to take a walk through the rainforest to see the ancient Huon Pines the area is known for. I was happy to feel the forest around me and to clear that yucky energy I felt on Sarah's Island.

135

For years my friends have "cleaned me up" when I return from my travels because I have tended in the past to pick up "bookies" or discarnate beings. Because it crossed my mind, I said a little prayer to shake off whatever I had picked up, and to help them on their way.

I moved quickly through the forest to get ahead of slower-moving visitors, looking for a quiet spot to sit a moment and just feel. I was soaking up the energy of *Life* that radiates from these trees as I walked — until I felt "them."

I was drawn off the path into a very small clearing surrounded by these old-soul trees. As I sat quietly and tuned in, I could feel the presence of more than just the trees. "They" were there as well. I could feel the deeply sacred presence of another Aboriginal group consciousness. They had been waiting for me.

I bowed in reverence and connected with them on a soul level. I wasn't sure if that works the same when they are in group consciousness, but it was the only way I knew to connect.

We did the work, exactly the same as on Hunter Island. I moved a little faster today, since I already knew where we were going. And I didn't want to miss the boat back to Strahan, since there wouldn't be another until tomorrow.

Even so, time slowed to a crawl and the presence was palpable. We were surrounded in an energy I can only describe as *grace*. It held us as we went into those places of trauma and unspeakable agreements, and gently released it from us all. The feeling was undeniable — a swell of gratitude and rightness washed over me.

When we were complete, I bowed deeply and quickly headed for the boat.

I don't know who's helping me so, but you have great timing, I thought as I reached the boat just before the gate closed.

Memories at the Museum

The next few days were pretty ordinary. Just driving through the Tasmanian countryside. Queenstown, described as "a testament to the brutal reality of Tasmania's mining past," definitely lived up to its description. The mountains were a "moonscape" because of the extreme tree removal and the excessive erosion. Unlike any place I've ever seen, it made me cringe for Nature.

Everywhere else just looked like rural towns and villages typical of the colonized Tassie. It was noticeable how many of the buildings everywhere were from the convict era. They were recognizable because they built with those large sandstone blocks.

I had been terribly disappointed when I arrived in Devonport on Sunday and the Tiagarra Aboriginal Cultural Center Museum was closed. It was supposed to have a great exhibit, specific to Tassie. So I hurried to arrive in Hobart during museum hours to see their Tasmanian Aboriginal exhibit. Weird thing — it was also closed. Not the museum, but that exhibit in particular. It wasn't closed for a day or weekend, but indefinitely, because it was being redone. I found it so peculiar that I wasn't being "allowed" to learn more about the Tassie natives from "mainstream" sources.

So with some time on my hands, I wandered through a few of the other exhibits. They had a fairly new one about Antarctica that I thought might be interesting. I was going to do a fairly quick walk-through, but I was suddenly riveted to a large screen. On it was an obviously very old film of a scientific boat going through the Southern Ocean en route to Antarctica.

I couldn't take my eyes off the screen. The boat was dwarfed as it moved up and down the swells and troughs. The waves were enormous, several times higher than the boat itself. I was stunned. This is what I was seeing in the weeks before going to Hunter Island. Waves so big you wondered how the boat stayed on the water. It was this sea, and these waves that had claimed my life before — I could feel it with all of my being. I could feel the silence as I sank under the water — to the silent depths. It was years later that it finally occurred to me that maybe Jackie had drowned with me.

Chapter 17

Tasman Peninsula

Early on during this trip I started to read *In Tasmania* by Nicholas Shakespeare. It was a way too-detailed account of the early settling of Tasmania, pieced together from letters from one of the author's rogue relatives who was involved in the early colonization. I had already read much about the murderous treatment of the island's native population. But this was my first peek into the stark, grim, often brutal world of the penal colonies.

So when I finally landed in Tasmania, the last place I wanted to see was Port Arthur, Australia's most intact convict site. It's just not the kind of history that I'd go out of my way for. And places like that — where people have been poorly treated — often gave me the creeps.

I knew how rock and earth could hold the traumas of the past. Several times I've visited spots of great tragedy, and could feel the despair thick like fog over the area. Even the Vietnam War Memorial in Washington, DC has this dense cloud over it from the sorrow and grief expressed by the bereaved loved ones who visit. And with a place like Dachau, the feeling is way

139

beyond sadness, more like the wretched hopelessness that comes from man's brutality to man. I imagined the prisons would carry a similar shroud. Basically, I'm repulsed by humanity's cruelty, and while I don't pretend it doesn't exist, I don't go out of my way to perceive the effects of it.

Besides, Hart had warned me to stay away from certain parts of Tasmania because of the many dark ghosts there. She thought I'd be too open. While I've never seen a ghost, I definitely wasn't looking forward to a first time. It was ironic that I'd be afraid of a ghost, yet I'd travel to the other side of the world to communicate with dead Aboriginal spirits. Go figure.

Hart had also recommended I spend two weeks on the Tasman Peninsula, which was an interesting place. It held onto its peninsula status by a narrow wisp of land called Eaglehawk Neck that connected it to the Forestier Peninsula.

According to the tour books, "It was here, during the convict penal settlement days, that savage attack dogs were chained from one side of the neck to the other within reach of each other to deter prisoners from attempting an escape by land." There was a bronze attack-dog chained there at the old outpost, a stark reminder of the past.

I had looked for a backpacker accommodation, like a youth hostel, somewhere on the peninsula, and found a large, well-populated place overlooking Port Arthur. Even the pictures of Port Arthur made me cringe, and frankly, sleeping next to all those tormented convicts was the last place I'd want to be.

So Eaglehawk Neck Backpackers it was! With its history, I was quite surprised that this was to be my "settling in" place for the next period of time. It was a one-bedroom house with a lounge, and kitchen. The composting toilet and the shower were outside. The owners lived right there and were quite friendly, offering bikes to borrow or a lemon from the garden.

I was the only person there most nights, so it was like having my own little house. It had a big picture window in the lounge that looked out on the bay. Across the narrow bay you could see the Tasman Peninsula, and it was obvious that many prisoners would have tried to escape this way if only they could swim.

But what really interested me out that picture window was a bunch of partly submerged rocks. I would often take walks down the road, along the water, and I would feel them there — a group of Aboriginal women spirits. Yet when I went down to the dock to sit with them, I was told to go back inside and keep reading. It seemed odd, but I had already flown to the opposite side of the world to meet a galactic portal — so obviously "odd" isn't enough of a reason to not do what I hear to do.

The rocks in the bay.

Fortunately, I had stocked up on food because getting groceries on the peninsula was pretty bleak. There was a café near the bronze attack-dog that offered coffee, pies and chips to the tourists. Not going to do me much good. But I did visit almost daily to use their internet.

And beyond the café was a great ocean beach. It was too chilly for swimming, but I visited regularly to walk in the surf.

Port Arthur Gift Shop

While driving around the Tasman Peninsula, I kept having these really moving episodes. I would have to stop and really let myself sink into nature and just listen. The sound of the wind through the eucalyptus trees was whispering to my soul. It was such a tactile hearing, such a visceral experience.

I eventually did stop at Port Arthur, attempting to get a glimpse of the place from a safe distance. Unfortunately, you can't see anything but the cafe and gift shop until you pay to go in. So I figured the gift shop would be safe enough. I just looked around, picking up a book here and there and reading a little bit. Yet the books were full of the ghosts of the past. Shipwrecks, treachery at sea and lots of convict stories, and they all told of the brutal and hard life of the prisoners.

And then there were the newspaper articles and the book about the recent massacre in 1996 — 35 people killed. So the place would have new ghosts too, but I couldn't feel anyone. It was a little sobering to imagine the tourists milling around looking for souvenirs and perusing the books, much as I was, and then hearing the gunfire and seeing people fall. Rarely have I read about such a tragedy while I'm walking around in the location of the event, especially one so recent. It was a little unnerving.

I was getting ready to leave and was curious about the nearby wall of photographs. As I looked closer I realized these were sent in by visitors who found unusual forms or apparitions contained in their photos. Imagine looking at your holiday photo and finding a ghost standing beside you. No, thanks. It seems there's a special nighttime ghost tour of the place and they encourage people to take lots of pictures hoping to find Casper the convict in the photo with their family. Not my idea of fun.

As I continued driving around the peninsula, it occured to me that most of the "historical" stuff for people to see was only around the colonialists and the convicts. There was almost no mention about the Tasmanian natives. I found that strange.

Blonde echidna

I also stopped at the Saltwater River Convict Coal Mine. I must have been going to see something else, because I can't imagine driving out of my way to see this place. The best part was seeing my very first echidna poking his way along in the bush. He was so cute — like a small porcupine with a long, narrow snout that he pokes around in the dirt looking for ants. I wish I had spent more time following him, because the historic site was both boring and disturbing.

The worst part was the underground cells. You could walk through a door into the side of the hill and go into them, but I was repelled by the pervasive sense of wretchedness and depravity. They felt so horrible I couldn't walk by fast enough. Yet I could still smell the dank and dismal hell hole. This was a place where men were put in solitary confinement. I could feel the barbarity. I could feel the resulting insanity. I scurried past and tried to quickly shut down my sensors. I thought back to the Port Arthur ghost pictures as I walked back to the car.

I'd hate to see a photo taken here, I thought and then cringed. I was so appalled. Later, I read somewhere that, "these cells must surely be one of the most horrific examples of penal life anywhere in Australia."

These accidental little forays into things that are distasteful to me were very infrequent, but were enough to make me steer clear of further exposure. Someone offered me a free ticket to tour Port Arthur while I was on the Peninsula and I turned them down. When I finally left the area to return to Hobart, I assumed I was through with the penal colonies for good. Hahaha —wrong again.

Chapter 18

Last Minute Assignments

Three days before leaving the US, I had had an astrology reading by phone with Don Cerow. When we were finished, he invited me to stay with him in Santa Cruz the night before I was flying out. I was surprised, but accepted, figuring it was just another moment of grace. That evening turned out to be very interesting and a total divine setup.

He was showing me the book he was working on regarding 2012 and the ending of the Mayan Calendar. He was including research about things that were going on in the world that were both hidden and detrimental for most of humanity.

Without even realizing I knew the word, I said, "Are you talking about the Illuminati?" He nodded and we went even deeper down the rabbit hole.

I'm not used to thinking about these sorts of things; in fact I rarely, if ever, know what's going on in the world. My friends, as a joke, used to ask me who was vice president or even president. It was just easier for me to not know, because I felt things so deeply. I remember reading a two-inch newspaper article about a riot in a prison years ago. There were some things in that article that were so unspeakably cruel I couldn't get it out of my head, or even speak about it. So I just stopped paying attention to most world events.

But what Don was sharing with me really stayed with me that night. I felt deeply like I was being given some instructions — if only I knew what they were.

I called Hart the next morning from Don's back patio and we had a very interesting conversation . . . .

"Hi, Hart, I needed to talk to you before I get on the plane tonight. Hope you don't mind," I said, knowing this would be the last call opportunity for a while.

"Now's a good time, what's up?" she responded.

"I had an astrology reading a few days ago with Don Cerow, you remember him from Massachusetts?"

"Yeah, I sure do."

"Well, he invited me to come stay with him before I catch my flight to Australia. He was showing me the book he is writing about this upcoming 2012 shift. And in the process of telling me things, I suddenly remembered the word 'Illuminati.' Now, I don't know why I know that word, but it's the men with the power and money that are controlling things the world over."

"Yeah, what about them?" she responded in her straightforward manner.

"Well, he was telling me some of what he's uncovered as he's been researching for his book. Pretty sobering stuff. Not what I usually like to think about or dwell on, but it has been very present in my mind since last night. I'm wondering if I'm supposed to do some agreement-breaking work with them."

"Ouch!" yelled Hart. "I just got a sudden jolt of energy, like a lightning bolt, when you asked that," she laughed. "I think that means yes." She went quiet for a moment and I knew she was tuning in.

"And you need to be someplace special while you do this work. Do you have your map handy?" Hart asked as she pulled out her ancient atlas with the map of Tasmania.

"Yeah, it's right here. What are you seeing?" I asked.

"You need to do this work out over the water somewhere." She paused, and I pictured her running her hands over the map feeling for energy. I'd seen her do this more than a few times.

"It's here, Storm Bay. Do you see it? It's off the coast quite a bit — look from Hobart going out into the deeper water and then south. Do you see it?"

I quickly followed her instructions and found the location. "How am I supposed to get out there?" I mumbled, seeing the words Storm Bay so far offshore.

"I don't know," chuckled Hart, "that's your problem."

After having a good laugh, we were silent for a moment as we both were feeling into the assignment.

"There's a silver thread that's going to help you. Just tune into that," she suggested.

"A silver thread?" I asked as I wondered what she was on about.

"It's coming from that metaphysical level that Michael and I found. I told you about that, right?" Hart inquired.

"Yeah, I remember . . . where it was really sparsely populated. The silver thread comes from there?" I trailed off, a bit confused.

"Yeah, I don't know what it is, but it's really strong, and it's important that you connect with that before you do this work," she emphasized. "Apparently it will give you access to star energy. That will enable you to infuse the Illuminati with a new vibration. Any idea how you're going to work with this?"

I sighed and thought for a moment. "No, not really. Not yet. Usually I don't know until I tune in and connect with the souls. I'm assuming there's some agreement with humanity that needs to be broken, but I won't know until I tune it. It usually goes so much deeper than I expect it to."

We chatted a bit more about my timing and about the work, but the really important information had landed. It felt really crucial on so many levels. I felt a slight bit of trepidation, but I knew deep within me that I would continue to be guided and shown what to do. I would be shown at a really deep level what the underlying issues were.

I was getting ready to say goodbye, when I remembered one more thing. "Hart, he also told me something else that's interesting and a bit concerning," I went on.

"Oh yeah? What did he say?" Hart asked.

"He said that October 13th would be very intense," I continued. "That I would hit a point of terror that regenerates or reenergizes something new — like hitting a hidden vein."

"Oh, being terrified doesn't sound like fun," Hart responded. "Let me take a look at it." Hart was quiet as she was tuned in, but my mind was still racing.

"It looks like it's a part of you that you imprisoned and needs to be freed up so it can express — a wild part. The rest of your trip hinges on how well you go through that moment," she suggested.

"Oh — sounds important. I'm wondering if it makes a difference where I am on that day," I pondered aloud.

"Where were you thinking of being?" she asked.

"I'll have been there several days by then. After Hunter Island I'm heading down to Hobart through the western part of the state."

"Well, Sue, there's a peninsula near Hobart. Let me find the name" she paused. "Here it is — the Tasman Peninsula. It feels like it's important for you to go there for a while. Maybe even a couple of weeks. My map is too little, so I can't see what's there. Can you tell me some of the place names? Of towns or landmarks?" she asked.

"Sure can, Hart. There's the Port Arthur penal colony?"

"No, yuck, that has awful energy," she groaned.

"How about Nubeena?"

"No."

"White Beach?"

"No."

"Eaglehawk Neck?"

"That's it," she exclaimed, "You need to spend some time there," she suggested before getting quiet. "But there's another place to go, down near the bottom of the peninsula. I can see where Port Arthur is — it's to the left of that. Do you see anything there?"

"Okay," I replied as I was rustling the map around. "There's a place called Remarkable Cave?"

"No, that's not it, but it's close."

"Well, right there is Maingon Bay and Cape Raoul. And further out is Storm Bay, where I need to go to do the Illuminati work."

"It's Maingon Bay, Sue. You need to go down to the beach there and put your feet into the water." She paused. I can feel her testing as she goes. "It's interesting, but I can't tell you why you need to go there."

"Okay, I should be able to do that. I've done stranger things without knowing why." I laughed.

"You sure have, Sue. You're really good at it." She paused for a moment before adding, "I don't feel anything bad happening at that bay, so I wouldn't worry if I were you."

"I know, Hart. I've gone through lots of things that people would find terrifying and it's no big deal. I'm just gonna trust that it'll be okay. After all, I didn't drown with the fisherman on the way to Hunter." We both laughed.

"Yeah, I think you'll be able to handle whatever comes your way," Hart added. "And I feel there's some sort of protection traveling with you. I think it's that Aboriginal group consciousness you picked up when you were crossing the Bass Strait. Be sure to let me know what happens."

"Don't worry, you'll be the first to know."

Chapter 19

Freeing My Primal Self

After a few days of rain, I was really happy to get out in the sun and fresh air. I was taking a look at Remarkable Cave before heading to Maingon Bay. The views were spectacular, overlooking a sandy white beach from the top of a very tall bluff. Judging by the number of surfers down in the waves, this was obviously a great spot. They probably account for all six cars in the car park.

Steps led to a viewpoint at the bottom, a bluff towering overhead. It was fascinating to see how the two caves had eroded out from under that rocky headland. As I stood there watching the waves crashing through the caves and then subsiding — I began to experience being timeless — not my body, but "me" — before the creation of form. It was a glimmer of the galactic formulating consciousness — that which created the earth and all its inhabitants. I felt a huge overwhelm — that feeling of pure spirit — and tears of gratitude welled up in my eyes.

I was well aware that I had a date to be somewhere. I had an appointment with primal terror, and I didn't want to miss it. So I pulled myself together and bounded back up the stairs. I looked around the area and could find no way to get down to the water. I could see the surfers out there, but no trails or steps anywhere.

So I went back and took a closer look at the map on the information sign for the area and my heart sank. The sandy white beach below was on Remarkable Bay, and Maingon Bay was out beyond that.

Okay, I think slowly. *What now?*

As if on cue, a ranger drove up. We had a nice little chat, and he directed me to the Mount Brown Trail. It was back up the road a piece, and would take me to the Maingon Blowhole and beyond. He thought if I walked past the blowhole, there was a place where I could get to the water. "Just be careful around the blowhole," he warned, "the edges are fragile."

So I grabbed my day pack and headed out. It was a sandy track that was easy to follow through the dense vegetation. It was spring here and the flowers were already starting to bloom. After the morning sprinkle, I could see that, other than wildlife, I was the only one on this trail. It was just a few kilometers to the blowhole, a nice easy walk, even with the undulating hills.

At first the bushes were close in and over my head, but as I continued, I moved into the stubbier grasses. This gave me a wonderful vista of the sea. I could see land off to the right — presumably Cape Raoul — otherwise just open sea. It was still a bit cool, and the sun was playing hide and shine. Perfect for a slightly strenuous hike.

I was remembering the astrologer saying that today would be a terrifying day and that I would be reconnecting with a primal part of myself. It was hard to imagine. Would I recognize it if I saw it? I laughed at my naiveté and willingness to wander to the ends of the earth to accomplish something I can't really imagine or name.

As I walked, I realized how amazing this is, me walking through the bush on a path that is not well traveled, by myself. I rarely felt comfortable walking in remote areas unaccompanied. I guess I've lived in the U.S. too long or heard too many stories. Or maybe it's just that I feel how alone and vulnerable I am. No one really knows where I am most of the time. But today I didn't hesitate or feel uncomfortable about it. Unusual.

As I neared the blowhole, there was an additional sign placed in an odd location, again reminding people to stay back. And if it wasn't for that sign, you wouldn't even notice that the path turns left and straight ahead is the blowhole. No railings or barricade — it would be so easy to walk right into the opening without realizing until you fell.

I followed the trail left, straining a bit, trying to see down into the gash. It was just a slit in the ground, maybe 20 feet long and a few feet wide. The edges had vegetation right up to the edge, and then just sloped right into it. It was impossible to see into the opening, but the noises coming out of it were terrifying. I could hear the waves thundering into the underground tunnel that had burrowed deep below the land on which I stood. I could hear the roar, the crash and the resulting splash. Yet even on tiptoe, I couldn't see the slightest spray.

My mind reeled at the thought of how deep it was, and of the possibility of someone slipping on the crumbling edges and falling in. A death sentence for sure — and the body would never be recovered. Remembering it's the 13th and my terrifying day, I took a few steps back and scurried on down the trail.

Maingon Blowhole on the Tasman Peninsula, Tasmania

I continued on the trail over the next rise and the next, hoping to see a way down to the water soon. Finally I saw what the ranger had described. The land was no longer sandy but had become rock, sloping fairly gently until it reached the water.

But wait, where's the beach? How am I going to do this?

"Hart!" I yelled. "You and your 'Put your feet in the water, Sue'," I mimicked with a laugh. I headed downhill, and then paused to watch the water. I could see it rising and falling — not like waves over a shallow beach. No, it was more like massive volumes of water moving up and down next to a cliff face.

I can't get my feet in the water there, I silently whined. *There must be a better place.* So I continued on the path to the top of the next rise.

"That's not getting any better," I mumbled, seeing the land rising again.

I turned around, and slowly walked back and down the rocks towards the water. This wasn't so steep, but I walked carefully nonetheless. As I neared the water I stopped and just stared.

Go sit down over there, take off your pack, remove your shoes. It was one of those "thoughtless thoughts" I had, so I followed the suggestions.

I was still quite a way from the water's edge and could watch — the water rise up and sort of spill over the cliff edge. And then it would sink. Swell and sink, swell and sink. And with every swell, there would be some water getting onto the rocks. Sometimes it was a big crashing wave, sometimes it was just swirling water spilling over. The crashes seemed to come in cycles, a few big ones, and then a few swirls.

Watching the water rise and fall, I realized this was an immense volume of water — not like a gentle wave on the beach — not even like a big wave on the beach. Having seen some of Tassie's rocks and cliff faces, I *knew* this was a steep cliff with water just barely cresting the top. Farther along the rocks, the waves were actually causing big crashes and splashes. Beautiful to watch, but I wasn't going near them.

As I sat and observed this water, I grew more and more terrified. I got such a deep gut feeling — face to face with the immense power of nature. Primal. I felt so insignificant. I knew a rogue wave could come along even where I was sitting and wash me away never to be found again. It's not something I would normally have considered, but the day before I had read about a scientist, working on a nearby island, who was lost this very way.

I sat there utterly petrified. I knew I needed to get my feet in the water, and it looked like an impossible feat. I could feel this raw, intense power, this primal aliveness.

And then I did the only thing I could think of. I pulled out my lunch and started to eat. It was amazing. As soon as I did this familiar thing, I wasn't afraid anymore. I felt safe — absurdly safe — like somehow doing something civilized or routine would in some way protect me from nature unleashed.

It made me laugh. And I thought about all of us humans — going about our day, feeling safe, invincible, protected, civilized. But we could be destroyed in an instant — by storm, flood, fire, and earthquake — so many things.

We set up our lives in a way we think will keep us safe and protected. And then we do anything necessary to keep the status quo — to keep things from changing. Humans hate change, they hate insecurity or the unknown, and they hate uncertainty. And so they construct a false sense of safety by creating a reality they can believe in. Rich or poor, their story — of family, job, lifestyle — gives them a sense of things being okay. Not that it really protects them, but it allows them to believe they're protected. No wonder so many people I encounter are entrenched in their comfort zones. I understood this because I had been there so much of my life.

I sat in the sun and enjoyed the warmth. I thought these thoughts and watched the rising and falling waves for an hour. I could feel the water's wildness, its aliveness. I could feel the intense power of not only the water, but the earth, the air, the sun. I could feel their primordial power. Unharnessed. Unforgiving. Uncivilized. Gorgeous — and terrifying.

And then I was jealous. I wanted to be that alive, to be that free, and to embody the primal. I didn't want to be a scared human afraid to do anything. I realized how fear had taken my life — how I had traded my *Life* for a false sense of security. I was filled with a desire to be totally alive and to be free — to feel fully and to be me.

I suddenly got up and headed toward the water, determined to complete my mission. I had noticed one particular rock that rose up higher than the others and created a foot-high bench. It was twenty feet from the cliff edge, and the cresting water would mostly just swirl around the base. *I'll sit on that bench rock and get my feet wet*, I think silently.

"I want to be alive and free," I yelled into the air — to the sun — to the water.

"I can do this," I proclaimed as I stomped my feet.

Filled with passion and life, I headed for the bench rock, observing the water. The waves caused big splashes and seemed to come in three's, so I kept watching — swirl, swirl, swirl, wave, wave, wave, swirl, swirl . . . I walked closer. I felt braver, I knew I could do this. It felt like my life depended on it.

Finally I moved swiftly toward the bench, keeping my eye on the water. I didn't make it to the rock before the water crested, but the swirl reached up and covered my feet.

Yeah, my feet got wet! I was thrilled as I took a few steps back. But because I didn't sit on the bench, I felt like I may have cheated.

I can do this; that wasn't so scary, I silently encouraged myself before heading back down to the bench rock.

I was almost there when the sea suddenly roared and reached up out of itself with a gigantic wave cresting over the edge. Instinctively, I turn and ran. I looked back just in time to see the bench rock completely engulfed in water.

Hmmmmm . . . That was one that would have washed me away for sure, I thought solemnly. Then I laughed, *Oh, I think these wet feet are good enough — I'm not going to push my luck.*

I scurried back up to my pack and shoes. As I re-shoed myself, I marveled at how different it feels — to be alive and present rather than being afraid and trying to protect myself.

Before starting the climb back to the path, I stopped to do the gyrating infinity symbols, noticing that it was now happening in 13 spots — the 2nd chakra, the primal piece had been added. I smiled and knew this initiation was complete.

As I climbed, I began to look at the cactus growing in the rock crevices. The orange and fuchsia flowers had already started to bloom and the rocks were covered in orange lichen. The color combination was gorgeous, so I stopped to take a picture.

And then I felt "them" — I felt the silence, that sacredness that had come over me on Hunter and again among the Huon Pines. I sat down and felt deep into myself. I could feel "them" surrounding me.

I started the Ho'oponopono with the earth, all creatures, the air, the water, and the spirits of this place. I could feel *grace* surrounding us all. And then we broke the agreements to cause suffering to each other. Again, I felt the deep relief, the freedom, and the celebration — for them and theirs, and for me and mine.

We sat together for the longest time. In harmony. In appreciation. In gratitude.

Turn Up the Wattage

Life is passion — it is energy and aliveness — it is meant to be creative and expressive. We are Creation expressing itself. As we try to fit into the culture and all that it dictates, we have repressed the natural, primal life force so it is a fraction of its true potential. And in the process, we have cut ourselves off from our passion, and from ourselves. After that, passion is only allowed out on certain occasions or certain circumstances. Otherwise it's considered too unruly or unbridled for polite company.

Aliveness unleashed makes people uncomfortable — it's too uncontrollable, unpredictable, and unmanageable. It's why we try to dominate and tame nature — it is unbridled *Life* and passion unleashed. It is wild and immense, and expressive — full of the power of *Life* — Creation in whole expression. We have in effect taken our 100-watt selves and dimmed our essence to run on only five watts — a dribble of the life force and creative brilliance available to us. When we occasionally start letting in more wattage, we get afraid because of the magnitude, the radiance, the magnificence we feel moving through us — so we turn down the dimmer switch to stay in our comfort zones and fit in.

There are numerous examples throughout history of individuals who, for whatever reason, dared to allow more juice through their systems. Einstein and Tesla are well known, but few people have heard of Walter Russell and his amazing body of work. (There's a good overview in *The Man who Tapped the*

Secrets of the Universe, by Glenn Clark.) All great geniuses, but also great humanitarians — Mother Theresa, the Dalai Lama, Gandhi. The truth is when we allow *Life* to inhabit us fully, what starts coming through is brilliance, divine inspiration and creation expressing.

Jean Houston, a forerunner in the human potential movement, said in many of her lectures . . . We are all naturally like Stradivarius violins, yet we only play like we're plastic ukuleles.

Chapter 20
Seeding My Mind

With Maingon Bay and Hunter Island behind me, the future was open. It looked like I would be settling down in Eaglehawk Neck for a few weeks unless something changed. After returning the car, I was happy to start moving slower and covering less ground — by foot or bike from now on.

Finally, it was time to pick up the book Hart had insisted I bring, *Voices of the First Day*, by Robert Lawlor. It didn't take long to realize that something really interesting was going on. That I would be covering way more ground than before — but just in my mind.

As I read, I suddenly *knew* things I'd never known. I would feel new ideas swirling in my being. They would meet up with other information or ideas that I had been carrying for a while — possibly years or lifetimes. The concepts would start synthesizing into thoughts I'd never thought. It was a fascinating process, unlike anything I'd experienced before.

Tasmanian Aboriginals

One of the most interesting chapters in the *Voices* book was about the Tasmanian Aboriginals. Through research, it was discovered that the Tassie group had undergone a major shift 4,000 years earlier than European intrusion: in the ways they ate, dressed, and used fire. This shift was not seen in the Australian Aboriginals.

After the shift, they quit using bone tools to make clothing and would have only a small skin around their neck — obviously not providing the warmth needed in such a southerly climate. They ceased eating scale fish, even though the middens indicated they had been eating it earlier. And they stopped using fire extensively, and began using it only for ceremony and cooking meat. The speculation was that they were re-adhering to the ancient spiritual directives upon which they were designed, after having gone through a slow transition away from them.

The research suggested that the Tassie group could easily be the earliest, oldest people on the planet, and that the Australian group might have migrated from Tassie. It's not what is traditionally thought or taught, yet I felt that he was onto something worth considering. I pondered this as I traveled, and sensed that the Tasmanian natives were designed differently from the other humans on the planet — like an heirloom seed.

I remembered the deep essence of the land that I first noticed when I arrived here, and the distinct wildness I could feel then — and had been experiencing throughout my travels. And I pondered the idea that they were designed to keep everything as it was on the first day, and how they felt so deeply connected — almost inseparable — from the land.

This was such a different design from the White European tribe — which seemed to be constructed with an inborn need to expand, perfect, and explore, to make the world a smaller place. Unfortunately, as a tribe, we are generally deeply disconnected from the earth, and have been expressing some hugely negative traits — aggression, greed, control, genocide. I would eventually come to understand this difference in makeup more clearly and also to see how its negative expression was unintentional in the design.

Kali Yugas

I had never heard of Kali Yugas before until reading about them in *Voices*. The yugas are enormous cycles that occur over vast expanses of time. The basic idea is that humanity will gradually evolve until we reach a golden age, and then the decline will begin. The Kali Yuga is this deteriorating cycle until we destroy ourselves — again. As I read, I *knew* that we had destroyed ourselves several times already. Atlantis and Lemuria are relatively well-known examples, but I knew there were more. And I *knew* we were heading that way again.

I was so depressed and distraught that I called Hart from the beach . . . .

"I'm reading about Kali Yugas. Have you ever heard of them?" I asked despondently.

"Yeah, I have. What does he say about them?" Hart asked.

"He says we've destroyed ourselves seven times. That we go through a 60,000-year period that includes rising up, a golden age, declining into depravity and eventually destroying ourselves again." I offered.

"That's what I've read and it does feel true," Hart responded.

"It feels like we are heading that way. It makes me so very sad," I said quietly.

"I know, it doesn't look too good for humans the way we're going," Hart replied.

"I hate that idea," I confessed.

"Yeah. Me too, Sue."

"For so long, I've had such a deep sense that humanity is on the verge of this tremendous quantum leap. I can barely believe that it makes sense to destroy ourselves again. For what? To start all over? We're so very close." I felt deeply into my gut before continuing. "I hate the idea of cycles."

"Well. Sue, there are also spirals — cycles that are moving gradually upward," Hart offered.

"So in a spiral — every trip around, we raise ourselves a bit higher?" I asked, thinking back to Don Beck's talk of Spiral Dynamics at Mystery School.

"Yep, that's the idea," Hart replied.

"Are there any prototypes for breaking through this cycle?" I wondered.

"Not that I know of, Sue."

"Lawlor says the Tassie Aboriginals survived an ice age and two Kali Yugas. There's the evidence of possibility," I offered.

We're quiet for a moment and I watched the waves hitting the rocks. Finally, quietly, I proceed, "I actually don't think we get destroyed this time, Hart." I pause as I feel a surge of hope. "I get a sense that we make it through this time without having to totally crash and burn. It feels to me like there's enough consciousness emerging on the planet that we get through this

— maybe not totally unscathed — but it doesn't feel like we need to completely annihilate ourselves."

"Sue, I feel the same way. I'm glad you can feel it, too."

"Thanks, Hart. I'm so glad I'm not crazy, or at least not the only one." We laughed.

From then on, as I read, I felt a sense of hope, regardless of what the Kali Yuga scenario was presenting — I felt a sense of purpose and a sense of rightness.

Messages from Beyond

I would look out into the bay outside the big picture window in the lounge, and I *knew* that out there with all those rocks were Aboriginal women spirits. I felt they were waiting patiently for me to listen. Yet when I wandered out to get a bit closer and tune in, I was told to go back inside and read the book, that the communication was happening just fine. Both times I laughed and continued my reading.

I would read and then pause and ponder, and then read again. And I would make notes in my journal for the really interesting bits, or things I didn't want to forget. Normally I would only write in my journal once a day. But so much was coalescing in my brain, and it was all so interesting and exciting, that the journal was always open beside me.

One night something interesting happened. I didn't recognize it at the time. But in the morning my first thought was, *what the frig was that? What happened last night?*

I opened my journal to the twelve pages I had written. As I read them, I was astonished. It was like a collage of many things I'd been pondering — during this trip and through life, but also some things I had never ever considered. It was threads from my own thoughts — woven in patterns and textures that were obviously not mine. I was stunned.

Well, that isn't something I'd write — because it's something I don't know, I thought, staring at the page. I didn't think about it much that day. In fact, I didn't think about it for several days.

Finally, on my last day in Eaglehawk Neck, I sat at Pirates Bay writing in my journal and thanking the spirits of place and the Ancient Ones for working with me. *A lot has shifted in my consciousness. It seems so subtle — until I see how radically the landscape inside has changed. I wonder if they want to tell me anything this last day . . . .*

Good work, thank you. You look for a final word, but it's too soon to ask for that. Be patient and continue to listen and hear. Some will travel with you to Flinders. We have prepared for you there.

Thank you for your willingness to hear and be moved. To feel who and what we are — not simple, not primitive, not ignorant. A consciousness from beyond this place — and from this place. We were able to integrate the Dreamtime and form — there was no solid boundary between them. You are learning the same. You can feel the truth of that in your heart.

There is much more to tell you — to show you — in the place where you can hear. There is much you can do to change the pattern — there can be a new pattern. Now is the era of the pattern-breakers within humanity. You have been placed with them and not with us so you can do this work. "It gives you the right," as you say.

We give you the memory of what's possible — both as a way of being, and also as a new pattern for humanity. We are the prototype for a new outcome, and much work needs to be done. But you are not alone in this. There are many in both form

and consciousness who are focused on this new — rivulets of creation spawning off the river.

You needn't ask about others now. That will come in time. For now, be joyous at your part — and know your strength and the power you carry.

Chapter 21
Storm Bay Assignment

One of my last-minute assignments was to take a boat ride out onto Storm Bay. I knew the work I needed to do there was *so* important that there was no way I would avoid it, even if I had to rent a kayak and paddle myself out. I had been searching the internet for a way to get there, without any luck.

When I finally returned to Hobart, I went to the wharf and asked about options. I discovered that the only boat going out through Storm Bay is the one taking tourists on the Port Arthur tour — and only because it has to cross the bay to get there. I was going to have to pay too much and go back to Port Arthur and spend the afternoon there. Just what I didn't want to do. If I thought I physically could have handled it, I would have opted for the kayak.

The night before the compulsory tour, I shared my room with the backpackers from hell. The mother was busy in the kitchen cleaning toxic chemicals out of something that had spilled in her car. The little girl was noisy and nosey, and demanded my pillow and blanket because they were more fun than hers. The relatively normal sister kept trying to talk some sanity into the other two. And all three of them snored! I didn't get much sleep.

As I lay awake, I could feel my apprehension. I knew it was time to work with the men with power and money, but I had no idea how I would approach it or what I would do. I said a little prayer that night — for guidance and miracles.

Seasick on Storm Bay

I woke up with a terrible head cold. My head pounded and my sinuses filled to overflowing — a typical reaction when confronted with toxins. How fitting for the work I was about to do.

The weather was cold and windy, and the water was wild. As the boat plowed through the whitecaps, I tried to listen to the tour through my clogged ears. Mildly interesting, but by the time we got to the spectacular cliffs of Cape Raoul, I was curled up inside, blowing my nose and trying hard not to wretch. So many boat trips and this is the first time I get seasick!

How am I going to be able to do this work. Hart did say there was some silver thread from somewhere that would help me out this day. C'mon thread, I need some help, I sneezed as I had this thought. *Can you send me some of that star energy to help my body, too?*

I was curled up on a seat, not even looking at the stunning scenery. Every time I turned to look at the gorgeous cliffs and rock formations, my urge to puke just intensified. I had practically pushed a hole through my acupressure points, and I was just barely avoiding a barf.

I wrapped my cashmere scarf around my head, closed my eyes and hunkered down into the seat. I waited and felt until I could see which direction to proceed. Suddenly it became clear.

I'd like to connect with all the men with the power and money by any name — Illuminati or whatever. The guys that orchestrate wars, depressions, assassinations, and all manner of things that disregard the common man and his rights.

I'd like to connect to them all on a soul level. Whether they are alive now, have lived in the past, or will be living here in the future.

I can see that you guys have been designed for something, and you've been designed perfectly. (I can't believe I hear myself think that.) And then I felt it . . . .

You think you have been given the power and money to orchestrate things that benefit yourselves and your families — a little "me." But what you have really been designed for is to orchestrate amazing things that benefit a bigger ME. And I see my arms open wide in my mind to include all of humanity. *That's the ME you have been designed to benefit — the whole of humanity.*

So it's just a slight turn, a little glitch that has you utilizing your power and money for something so much smaller and self-absorbed than the amazing, glorious, magnanimous intention that is in your design. This is the expression for which you have been created.

As I explained this to them, I started to see it all so much clearer, in a way I would never have guessed.

I invite you to choose to make this slight turn in focus. Right now your littleness doesn't make you happy. You think it does. You avoid feeling deep inside, because if you go there, you will feel that emptiness, that soul sickness. Your actions now keep you disconnected — from yourselves and everything — and you will never be happy that way.

But if you would allow yourselves to connect to all that you are and to all that is you, you would find you have a very special function within humanity. To orchestrate this quantum leap in consciousness for all of humankind. You have been given the funding. You have been given the networks. You have been given the ability to move mountains.

Fulfilling this function will be so much more satisfying than anything you are doing now. It will open the doors of your hearts and your minds — to happiness, to peace, to connection, to true purpose. Something that all of your money and power has not been able to give you. I paused for quite a while, looking deeply and feeling my way through.

I would like to connect to all souls who have ever been manipulated, controlled, injured, enslaved, abused, disrespected, disregarded, or caused to suffer in any way by the activities of these men with the power and money. All souls, whether on the earth now, previously, or in the future.

The Universe is wholly beneficent and fully harmonious. It is impossible to be a victim of anything without having made some agreement on some level of being. These agreements can be conscious, unconscious, karmic, through ignorance or acquiescence, and also implied.

Agreements through acquiescence are when the soul <u>believes</u> the other party has the right and power to injure it in this way. But each one of you is a sovereign being. You have the right and the power to choose your experiences. You have the right and the power to break these agreements if you so choose.

Both sides have honored these agreements, but it is more loving to break these agreements and free both sides from the damage or effects, and from carrying the karma. Either side can break these agreements, and both sides are then free. If only one side breaks the agreement, both sides are still free.

I invite you all, whether the victim or the perpetrator, to break these agreements in their entirety, past, present and future. If you are not yet ready, this invitation will remain outside of time and space eternally.

You may access it when you are ready. All that's needed is to have a thought of being free, finding joy, being happy, blessing another. Even a tiny wish for your experience to be different than it is now.

I pray that you all be blessed with whatever miracle you most need. And I disconnect with you all.

Throughout all of this, I coughed and sputtered and blew my nose. I stayed as present as possible, as I swayed with the boat trying desperately to hold my breakfast.

This was the first and only "out-of-time agreement-breaking session" that I couldn't feel the clear falling away of the dross. It could have been my head cold and seasickness. But it felt like there was something more to do. I racked my brain, but it wouldn't come to me. Little did I know that I would be waiting years. Watching and waiting to see what the next piece would be — it did eventually come a decade later.

But my job wasn't to try and figure out how the work had landed. I was aware from the onset that I would never really know for sure. Never be able to prove it. My job was to follow the sense of rightness and to do what was being asked. And to be willing.

Obviously Hart was playing a big part in the guidance needed for my moving around and knowing some of what I was encountering. But it was my sense of rightness that was the final yeah or nay on my choices, and it was my deep internal knowing that guided me through these encounters with souls.

The boat finally landed at Port Arthur and I was so happy to be there — just to get off the boat. The land was swaying as I walked up the path on this dismal, dreary day, but inside the sun was shining.

> *Author Aside* – *You may, as you read this book, accept the invitation I just offered and break any of these agreements, from your past, present and future. Just close your eyes, take a deep breath, and ask that it be so. Thank you.*

Port Arthur Blessing

We had three hours to look around before the long bus ride back to Hobart. I figured I could easily wait that out in the café. I had some warm and nourishing pumpkin soup and hot tea while I tried to warm up and regain my stomach. It worked well, and I enjoyed the quiet while the rest of the tour was out in the cold. But as time passed, I finally got up and entered the actual site. What else was I going to do for two more hours? I've already perused the gift shop. Better I just walk the grounds and avoid the nasty places.

Indoors, before you enter the site, they give you some actual history of the convicts who ended up here. I stopped and read about them all and was appalled to realize that these weren't all criminals. Sure, there were a few murderers and such. But most of these convicts were the desperately poor, caught in petty crimes like stealing a handkerchief or a loaf of bread. Doing what they needed to do to survive or take care of their family during really desperate times in Great Britain. Many were woman and children.

As I continued to read the storyboards I started to get the picture. These "criminals" were transported to the opposite side of the world via a long and torturous boat ride that many didn't survive. They would do seven years of hard labor, and when they had completed this sentence, it was up to them to figure out how to get back home.

Basically the British had enslaved their own poor and used them to build the colony.

What the hell makes Britain so civilized? I wondered as I went out into the dreary weather. *It seems that their barbaric ways are hidden under a veneer of civility.*

Outside, the first stop was the site of the old café where the 1996 massacre happened. They've completely gutted the place and torn down the roof. Only the stone walls and a gravel floor remain. The wind blew through the frameless windows and made me wrap my scarf tighter around my aching head.

As I walked the grounds, I started to notice how amazing the old ruins were, the buildings being built of large cut sandstones piled high in multi-storied buildings. It was easy to see the marvelous workmanship, and also to imagine the back-breaking work involved. They would be beautiful if not for the price paid by the human soul.

I had seen these large cut stone buildings throughout Tassie, and now I was realizing they were all built in the convict era by the prisoners. Apparently the sandstone was local and readily available, and ". . . the state provided the added incentive of cheap convict labor . . ."

A few times I got closer to the actual cell blocks, but always felt gently pushed away. Yet there were many buildings I could enter and look around. It wasn't like those living museums where they attempt to recreate the place to look, feel, and smell as it might have in its day. On the contrary, the buildings were stone-cold empty inside, holding nothing reminiscent of its earlier use. And even much of the energy had somehow been purged.

I was relieved as I finished walking past the last of the buildings and headed through a garden. I could wait out the last half hour over a cup of tea.

You guys can stop following me now, I heard my mind say. *What?*

I stopped and wheeled about. *Who am I talking to?* I asked inside, but already I knew the answer. I knew they were around me. Yet I didn't feel frightened. I actually felt sorry, deeply sorry. I wouldn't have even noticed them if I hadn't suddenly responded to them with an un-thought thought. But now that I knew, I realized there's something for me to do.

I started walking again, feeling a bit nervous, yet also trusting that somehow I'll know what to say. I relaxed and began to feel into the situation. I could sense their confusion. They didn't know where else to go or what else to do. It seems that the brutality of their lives have distanced them from their soul knowing. So now they were just lost.

All right you guys, here's the deal,. I started to talk to them directly in my mind. *You suffered deeply before you died. I'm terribly sorry about that*. Then it occurred to me that this wasn't much different than what I'd been doing with the indigenous spirits. So I started again.

If I or any of my ancestors have wronged or caused you or any of your ancestors suffering, I'm deeply, deeply sorry. Please forgive me. I love you. Thank you. I paused and could feel a gentle softening as that sunk in.

The agreement you made to suffer, the agreement you made on a soul level that brought you to this place, to this life of misery — you can break that agreement. You have the right and the power to break this. You can break it now and it will release the effects of this life from your soul memory. And you will no longer be bound — to this place, to this memory, to the other parties involved.

I waited quietly. I could feel the disbelief, followed by the bonds beginning to break. I could feel the ripples begin to expand through consciousness as a result. I had felt this many times, but each time is so moving. My eyes started to fill. I paused to wipe my freely running nose.

You are free to leave this place whenever you wish. There are those who will come to help you, I said internally, not really knowing who or what these helpers were — only certain that they existed. I was walking through a grove of trees by now and intensely feeling the natural world nourishing and supporting us all. I was filled with gratitude for this moment; I felt blessed with this encounter. And I could sense the relief and gratitude as the prisoners accepted their release.

Within me, I add, *I extend this invitation to all the convicts who ever lived here at Port Arthur, or in Tasmania, or Australia. They can accept it when they are ready.*

A sense of completion filled me; I knew I was finished here. It's hard to believe I was trying so hard to avoid this place and an encounter with the discarnate souls who were stuck here. As I walked back to the main building I noticed the sun was shining. I loosened my scarf and took a deep breath of fresh penal-colony air. I could even smell the spring flowers.

It was almost time to catch the bus back to Hobart and as I passed the photos of the guests and their ghosts, I started to laugh.

Uh oh, I thought to myself, *those nighttime ghost tours will never be the same.*

Chapter 22

A Lifetime of Questions

Throughout the years I've come to suspect that any question that's really asked will be answered. When I say "really asked," I mean that it's asked with an earnest desire for a real answer, not just an answer that supports the status quo. I don't know if it matters of whom or what the question is asked. I have directed my questions towards a great assortment of things — animals, sky, trees, inanimate objects, and divine beings. In fact it might work better when you ask nothing or no one in particular, and let them sort it out in the mail room.

I don't know what answers me. It could be God, or his helpers, or my dead relatives, or a general dynamic of fulfillment that makes up the Universe. But I am often aware that I'm being answered.

I've had very direct answers come in the most astounding ways. A line in a book, a song playing in my mind, something shows up on the news, the grocery clerk mentions something to the other clerk; sometimes someone will walk up to me and just say it.

There's a certain feeling that accompanies the answer, as if something within me says "pay attention, this is important." This is true even when I don't remember the question. And afterward I can remember that "special" bit of information but not really anything else that was said.

And when it's *really* important, one that you definitely don't want to miss, the feeling is intensified. The world slows down, sort of like when you're having an accident, or the lighting changes, or the world fades except for the messenger of your answer. Sometimes you can almost feel a dimensional shift, even though you have no idea what that would feel like.

I have to admit I don't always recognize an answer. And often it doesn't look the way I thought it might. Sometimes I'm shocked at how different the answer is from what I had hoped for, yet it is a thousand times more perfect than I would have come up with. Other times I take the response for granted and only later recognize that this was actually in answer to my request.

And regardless of what you requested: a piece of information, help with a problem, or why something is the way it is, an answer comes — in a second, a day or a lifetime.

I read that every book should have an overarching question and the answer that the author is providing. While thinking about what question my book would be asking, I realized I've been asking the same questions throughout my life. What's up with humanity? What can I do to help?

Earliest Memories of the Question

One of my earliest memories as a child about five years old was going out to the movies one night to see Lucille Ball in *Fancy Pants*. I only remember a single image from that movie, that of Lucille wearing the type of pants worn for horseback riding. I'm sure it was funny and entertaining and appropriate for a child my age.

Unfortunately, it was a double feature — *Fancy Pants* being followed by a movie about Marco Polo. Now I remember quite a few images from that movie I was obviously supposed to be sleeping through. There was a great horizontal wheel, perhaps a grinder of some sort, or maybe it pumped water into the fields. What stuck with me was the image of people chained around this great wheel like an animal would be in order to keep the great wheel turning. They were being whipped to keep them moving in spite of their obvious pain and fatigue — whipped by people who didn't care that the others were in agony.

I don't remember the question I asked that night at so young an age, or even if I asked one. Yet I carry that image to this day along with others that I've stumbled upon by accident. Some are unspeakable images, ones that I could never bring myself to speak of to another person because they were so upsetting to me. I avoided the atrocious as best I could. I stopped watching the news or reading the newspaper, and I was very careful about the movies I would see. But those images haunted me throughout my life. How could people treat other people so badly? How is it that someone's life was so lacking in value, much less respect or dignity? What was it in humanity that allowed such treatment to exist?

Reframe of the Same Question

As I got ready for my trip to Tasmania, a thought occurred to me — no, really a question. Why is the white European tribe like a pack of locusts on the planet? This question emerged from nowhere in my mind, but now that it was present, it was the one I would ask myself daily as I moved through this adventure. It felt like a new question, but looking at it now, I see it's the same question I've been asking since childhood. Seems like it has been the question of my life — one that was leading me closer and closer to my soul's purpose.

I had learned during my spiritual awakening that all the answers are available to us. So a question honestly asked was one the Universe was going to set about answering. And it certainly has done that.

Initially, this wasn't a question I expected an answer to, but in the end so much more surfaced than I could ever have imagined. I had been picking up the snippets, pieces, crumbs of an answer for all of my life, but on this trip and during the years that followed, I was finally beginning to get a sense of the answer that was coming. And yet, I still couldn't fathom how much my life was about to change.

Chapter 23

Asking for Help

Asking for help from people has never been easy. I didn't want to bother them or didn't have a way to repay them, or didn't want to seem weak, or didn't know who to ask — so many reasons not to.

So I was really happy when I started to realize that I have guides and helpers assigned to me for this life. Their job is to be helpful, but there is a limit to what they can do if I don't ask. They aren't allowed to interfere. So if I ask for help, they can give me way more help than if I don't. I discovered I could ask the angels, too.

Initially I felt a little silly making requests to something I couldn't see or hear or even feel. But I really didn't want to overlook any help available to help me move forward in my life. And when I started seeing things happening — good things and helpful things — in sometimes shockingly miraculous ways, I kept asking.

One of the most valuable things I stumbled upon in my unfolding was my favorite way to ask for help. It seemed that most of us have trouble accepting the help that's been given —

whether by our friends and family or by those invisible helpers. It started out simply . . . .

Please help me to receive all the help that I'm being given.

Some days it gets bigger . . . .

Please help me to receive all the love, blessings, help, healing, guidance, opportunities, clarity, motivation, inspiration, (fill in the blank), being given me this moment and every moment.

I would say this as I was driving to work each day — not to anyone or anything in particular. And I began to notice things being easier and flowing more smoothly in all areas of my life. I still ask this most days, and am so very grateful for the help I receive.

Chapter 24

Isn't There a Nine Somewhere?

Eaglehawk Neck was drawing to a close, and my only dilemma was where to go after Hobart.

"Hart, in a few days I'll be heading north. When we last talked, Sisters and Penguin were an eight out of ten. But I keep trying to get a ticket to go there, and I can't go. I don't know why I can't go, but nothing in me will let me head there," I whined.

"Okay, Sue, let me get out the map and have a look. Well, Sisters and Penguin are still eight's," she offered. "I wonder what the pro . . . ."

"Isn't there a nine somewhere?" I blurted impatiently.

"I don't know, Sue, give me some possible places."

"St Helen's?"

"No, still too many ghosts on that northeast coast," she said with a laugh.

"Launceston"

"No"

"George Town? Back to Devonport?"

"No. No."

"Well, I've been through all the towns that make any sense," I groaned. "Wait, I wasn't going to suggest it since it's been a no from the beginning, but what about Flinders Island?"

"That's it, Sue. That's a nine out of ten," Hart said with finality. "What is that place, anyway? I know you've mentioned it, but I don't remember the details."

"Flinders is off the northeast coast. You should be able to see it on the map. It's fairly big," I directed.

"There it is," Hart said.

"It's the place where they took the last full-blooded Aboriginals. After the Black Line failed to round them all up, the government appointed George Robinson as *Protector of Aboriginals.* He went around and talked to all the tribes to try and get them to cooperate. They were led to believe there would be a treaty with the colonists.

"But what happened was shocking. They took them all to Flinders Island to make them civilized and Christianized. They tried to make them like white folk — making them wear clothes and such. They weren't allowed their normal foods, they lived in cold brick buildings, and weren't allowed to wear the grease and ochre they used to decorate themselves and keep themselves warm." I offered what little I knew.

"Sounds horrible, Sue."

"Yeah, there were about 130 or so to begin with, all from different tribes. And in just over a decade, over 100 of them died from illness, disease, and homesickness," I continued.

"Oh, no!" Hart gasped.

"Finally the remaining ones wrote to the government and begged to be able to return to their homeland. They finally let the small group return to mainland Tassie at Oyster Bay, but they were still dying.

"Now up to this point the colonists were doing terrible things, like sending body parts from the deceased Aborigines back to England where they were on display — heads, feet, hands. I read they were even making coin purses or tobacco pouches out of men's scrotums." I cringed as I continued.

"The story is that Truganini, one of the last women alive, begged to be buried in a respectful way when she died. But what did they do? They hung her body in a museum for 75 years. It wasn't until 1976 that they finally let her be properly buried." I shook my head as I spoke. "Absolutely disgraceful."

"What a shame," Hart said quietly and we both paused.

"Oh, and by the way, Flinders Island is where Robert Lawlor lived when he wrote *Voices*."

"Really? That's interesting, Sue. We've checked out Flinders Island before. I wonder why you can suddenly go now," Hart pondered as she closed her atlas.

She was quiet for a moment and then added, "It feels like they really want you there. You're not going to heal anything. They are going to change the way you think — about the galactic formulating consciousness. Something had to happen in you before it could open up."

"Wow. This will be interesting," I responded, not knowing whether to be delighted or scared.

"This trip is turning out to be pretty fascinating, Sue. I'm so glad you're keeping me up to date."

"Well Hart, I have to keep you up to date or I won't know where to go." I laughed, even though I was being honest. If I had to find my way alone, it would have been a much different trip — slower for sure.

Chapter 25

Flinders Island

As I flew over to Flinders Island in that little plane, I was looking down at the water, and watching the white caps forming around each pile of submerged rocks. The internet claimed there were about 100 islands in the Furneaux group. I wondered how they determined the real islands from the wannabe's, because there were lots of rocks popping out of the water. No wonder this area was renowned for being a shipwreck graveyard.

The winds were shocking, but I was too intrigued by this little island to worry about the pilot's skills. He obviously had plenty of practice, because the "roaring forties" is something this place is known for. The views of the mountains and beaches as we were coming in were incredible. Looking back to that first moment of touching down, I had no sense of the impact this visit would have on the rest of my life, or how much time I would eventually spend here.

I was booked into the local cabin park, which was a stone's throw from the airport. This worried me a little until I landed and saw how tiny the airport was. It was the only budget lodging on the island, but was great compared to staying in a backpackers accommodation with strangers.

The cabin park also rented cars, but I was trying to conserve money, so I asked the owner, Gerard, about hitchhiking up to Wybalenna. Safety wasn't Gerard's concern, just the lack of cars traveling the roads — even the main roads. And the road out to Wybalenna would be worse. I found that hard to believe until I started driving there. (I hit really bad traffic one day — I saw four cars at once.)

So I decided I would rent a car every other day, from midday till midday. That way I could go somewhere every day and still have time to rest and write and even knit. And I would start tomorrow.

Today I would just walk the four kilometers along the beach track to go into town for groceries. So I headed down Bluff Road until I reached the beach, which was more of a big bay with one lone boat moored there. The sand wasn't pretty or nice, but there were some pockets of great little shells. I started to collect a few, but they were so sweet I picked up quite a pocket full. They were tiny and the most gorgeous iridescent green. Later, I would learn these were a favorite for the natives who made amazing shell necklaces with them.

There was an information sign posted along the track that paralleled the beach. It said the Aboriginals had walked this track when the white man was bringing them up to Wybalenna. As I walked through the trees, I wondered what that must have been like. They had celebrated a treaty, not a surrender. Now here they were — being taken from the land they belonged to and brought to a foreign place. The land of their ancestors, to which their consciousness is connected, is elsewhere. They must have felt lost — alone for the first time. They had their land and culture — the fabric of their being — taken from them. No wonder they were heartsick here and so many died. Their connection to what sustained them had been stolen. Once these musings finished, I tuned in more deeply, but didn't feel anything — no spirits, no group consciousness, and no messages — so I just enjoyed the walk.

This island was home to about 700 people. Even knowing that, I was shocked when I reached Whitemark, the main town for the whole island. It was so small — maybe a block long. And there was no traffic — only a car or two. The hotel and pub were obvious, as was Bowmans General Store, but I had to look a little harder to find the grocery store tucked around a corner. It, too, was small but surprisingly well-stocked.

***

Flinders is a long, skinny island — twenty three miles wide and thirty eight miles long. The roads were mostly dirt, and there's tons of wildlife. That was obvious by the amount of road kill.

It was easy to see wallabies and pademelons, the smaller cousins of the kangaroo, hopping along everywhere. Even more exciting was the occasional echidna by the road, and I even spotted a blonde one. I really wanted to see a wombat, but there were fewer of these, and they weren't often along the roads.

Because of the limited cell phone access on the island, I would not be able to communicate with Hart while I was here. She had been a major navigational help so far, so I might have been worried, but the sense of rightness filled in and I knew I would be fine.

Several days into my visit, I received an email from Hart with some comforting news. She felt that Flinders wasn't about me having an experience, but more about me being seeded with something — that I'll understand later. That felt right at the time, and a decade later, while reading my journal, I had a big laugh.

Yeah, I was seeded all right, and finally I have the perspective to understand with what and by whom.

Chapter 26

Wybalenna

In the morning I drove to Wybalenna, the location of the settlement where the indigenous people were taken after being rounded up on Tassie. It was a large grassy field with a chapel that had been refurbished to commemorate the spot. I was surprised at this idea, and wondered how the Aboriginals felt about being commemorated by a symbol of what was trying to control and convert them. Sad, really.

The only other building was the commander's house, which was very ordinary, but I enjoyed the iris blooming everywhere. As I walked through the grounds, I kept feeling around inside for any insights or communication, but did not feel anything.

Finally, I walked on the mounds that had been the "black men's houses." You could see the brick fragments among the pile of dirt and grass. That's when a tiny window opened. And for a split second, I could feel the deep despair and desolation of the people being held there. And then the window snapped shut, and the feeling was gone.

Even when I walked down the dirt road to the cemetery, I still felt nothing. No one talking to me, no group consciousness, no sacred feelings. The cemetery seemed mostly empty except for the concrete headstones the Europeans had placed on their family burials. And there was a single monument for the more than 100 Aboriginal people buried there.

It would be years later when I was able to see the 1993 video called *Black Man's Houses*. It was a documentary where they used a scientific device that sensed the soil and could tell whether the dirt had ever been disturbed. They used this throughout that empty-looking cemetery and located all the Aboriginal gravesites. Their findings matched up with the map of the cemetery kept by the settlement overseers. At the time, the local Aboriginal population and their friends fenced the cemetery and put markers on each and every grave. The most disturbing part was that — within days — the markers and fence had all been ripped out. That said more to me about the bigotry that they still had to endure even into the '90s.

When I left Wybalenna, I stopped in the cute little Furneaux Museum, and had a wander through. Most of the exhibits were maritime equipment or tales of the locals, but what I was delighted to find was an area specifically about the Tasmanian Aboriginals — finally.

It was a small room, and not well displayed at the time, but there was more to look at then I'd seen anywhere else. I have to admit, I learned more from the old pamphlet that Gerard had provided me about their history on Flinders. But at least the museum had a dedicated area. There were shell necklaces, old photos, and binders full of old letters — everything accessible for anyone to look at.

The shell necklaces were stunning. I was so impressed to think of these women collecting all those shells and processing them to clean out the prior owner. But the mariner shells needed to be cleaned in such a way to get that gorgeous green iridescence uncovered. Many of the necklaces used different types and colors of shells too — all small, and some downright tiny. And the combinations were so creative and beautiful. There would be hundreds of shells on each necklace. Later I would learn there were still women on the island using this ancient wisdom passed down from their ancestors.

Then I started to look through all of the old photos and found several of the mixed-race families who had lived on the island. Apparently in early 1800's, sealers came to the Bass Strait and would kidnap Aboriginal women as slaves and concubines. These photos were obviously from a later date, and showed the Aboriginal women dressed in European dress surrounded by a white man and a whole family of children. I looked at these women and wondered so many things. How did they adjust to their situation and manage to be so resilient? Did they always feel like captives, or did time and circumstance eventually allow them to settle into this strange life thrust upon them?

I also wondered about the children in the photos, and would years later meet many of their descendants. Some described to me how they were raised in an Aboriginal community on neighboring Cape Barren Island, yet were taught that the Tasmanian Aboriginals had all died — that they no longer existed. I couldn't even imagine what that would feel like to a young indigenous child — how confusing and even undermining for your sense of self.

> **Author Aside to all the original peoples of Tasmania and their descendants –**
>
> When I arrived in Tasmania in 2007, I had read and been told that all the Tasmanian Aboriginals had died, and I believed it. Even when I could see the evidence in photos of ancestors, I still would accept the "full-blooded" idea as if it made any real sense. I am delighted to now know the truth — that you are still here and you are many. I apologize deeply for my ignorance. I thank you for setting me straight.

***

As I drove back to the cabin park, I realized I wasn't on Flinders because of the Aboriginal history here. While it was interesting and appalling, I didn't feel anything pulling me to a deeper level — other than that momentary window into the suffering while visiting Wybalenna. Having that feeling open and close so quickly felt like a message — that the Flinders connection would be elsewhere.

So now, I didn't know why I was here. I wasn't even called to read the *Voices* book anymore. But I knew there must be some reason; after all, it was a "nine." And while it had been a no for months, I kept looking for a clue as to why Flinders had finally become a possibility. So each day I would head to a new part of the Island and just enjoy nature, feel into the day, and knit.

Chapter 27

A Life Changing Meeting

My first night on Flinders, after my walk to town, I had a
leisurely dinner and wrote in my journal. I would have stayed
in the whole night, but the toilet was in a separate building. I
was returning from there when over the trees I could see the
beginnings of a glorious sunset. Suddenly I decided to get a car
now and drive somewhere to be able to see it better.

"Hi, Sue, Do you need something?" Gerard asked when he
answered the door.

"So sorry to bother you, but would you mind if I hire a car
tonight? I'd like to go watch the sunset somewhere," I asked
with a sense of urgency that didn't make sense to either of us.

"Sure, that's fine. I'll go get one and bring it round to the
cabin." He was definitely a good-natured sort and didn't seem
annoyed at my request.

I had seen Walkers Lookout on the map, so I hurried there as
fast as I could drive on unfamiliar gravel roads. Without center
lines, I had to concentrate a little more on which side of the road
I was on. I kept looking over my shoulder to see if I would
indeed make the sunset or if it would fade without me.

197

The sky was getting decidedly blacker as I drove up the hill.

I think I've missed the sunset, but I'm here so I may as well see the view. I mused as I reached a parking area with a cell tower and shed. *Hmmmm, I wonder if I'm supposed to park here or follow that road up to the top.*

It doesn't look like much of a road and it's steep. I tried to imagine myself driving up the steep rutted track. That caused me a little queasiness, but I gasped at the thought that I might have to back down. *No, I don't think so! I'll just walk up.*

As I walked up the hill, I realized dark storm clouds now filled the sky in every direction. I zipped up my coat against the cold wind that was blowing. Looking off to the left I could see the mountain was being rained on. And to the right it looked much the same. As I crested the hill the wind hit me full force. I had to really lean into it to move forward.

The top of the hill was quite impressively the top. Not a large area, but nothing rose above it except for the metal tower that was fastened to the center. There were signs facing four directions to explain which peaks and islands you could see, but they were too weather-beaten to read. The wind whistled through the tower. There were also two rusty metal beams jutting out of the ground. Later I would learn there used to be a mine there.

My pace slowed as I started to walk across this place. The wind was intense, but I slowed for another reason. I had started to feel . . . something different. It was just a glimmer at first — the kind of glimmer I used to hurriedly brush away for fear of what I might discover. But I had learned to allow those inklings to reveal themselves.

I stopped as if listening; straining to hear a whisper beyond my range.

I closed my eyes and turned my head and listened closer. I could hear only the wind. Yet, the sacredness started to permeate my being. Softly at first. My edges were melting. I sank into the deep silence that asks no questions. In the stillness I recognized — there was another presence here. It felt immense and primal. I was so little and insignificant next to it, yet it was welcoming. I could feel it in every cell of my being. They were welcoming me. They were happy I was here. Their joyousness swept through me. I felt uplifted.

This must be another Aboriginal group consciousness, I thought, not recognizing that no other encounter had felt like this.

Hello. I'll bet you'd like my shells. I think these are the ones you used to use to make necklaces. I threw some shells in the air, not realizing how ridiculous I must sound. Why would these spirits want shells? Yet it was all I had to give.

I was ecstatic. I was filled with glee. I reached in my pocket and pulled out the shells and started throwing them in the air. I laughed. I cried. I felt loved. I was *so happy.* And they were *so happy.* A welcome, a celebration — a riotous, joyous celebration!

Then when I thought things couldn't be better, the most amazing thing happened. Right in front of me, a few hundred feet away, a single opening in the dark clouds allowed the sun to shine through making a cone of radiance. I knew it was a gift for me.

Walkers Lookout, Flinders Island, Tasmania

And yet the real gift was so much more. It would be two months until I began to recognize what I had met that night, and it would be years until the enormity of the gift would surface in my awareness. I would later share this message with friends:

"It was the most glorious yet mysterious and life-changing experience of my entire trip. I was greeted in an amazing celebratory welcome by something unknown. It felt immense and primal, yet gentle and sparkly, like star beings. Whatever I connected with there was different from the Aboriginal consciousness I frequently encountered on this trip, more akin to a circle of consciousness involved with creation."

Chapter 28

"We Gave You Wombats"

I found the people on Flinders very friendly, welcoming, and curious about what brought me there. When asked about my reasons for visiting, I tried to be as casual as possible. How do you describe this sort of quest without sounding a bit daft? I was called, I had a whim, a wild hair, I was having dreams of aborigines, I had a date with a galactic portal, or the galactic formulating consciousness invited me. All true, but none sounded normal, so I did my best.

I tried this out with the museum curator first, who wasn't fazed in the least but immediately offered, "You need to go to Healing Dreams." I thanked her for the suggestion, even though I couldn't quite tell what it was or why I'd want to go there.

But as I traveled and chatted, two more people said the exact same thing, "You have to go to Healing Dreams."

Mount Strzelecki, Flinders Island, Tasmania

Okay, already, I'll go, I thought. I was just happy to finally get some direction. So I headed south past Whitemark and onto the dirt road to Mt. Strzelecki. It was amazing to feel the mountain rising on the left side of the road, and to be able to look over the pastures to the right and see the ocean. Starting at sea level, that mountain rose to 740 meters (2,428 feet) and was quite impressive.

Healing Dreams

I drove up the drive marked Healing Dreams and saw a nice peach-colored wood frame house at the top of the hill. From the car park and the veranda, the views were stunning — across pastures and bush to the ocean — with Chapel Island rising in the distance.

I walked into the house, wondering if I needed to knock, and gave a little holler. The guidebook said it was a luxury accommodation, with spa offerings like massage. It was beautifully built with lots of gorgeous wood, and enormous windows that brought in the views.

A man emerged from a back room and introduced himself as David. I explained that all roads were leading here and he laughed. Then we realized we had talked on the phone just the week before when he booked my trip over here, so it felt like we were already friends.

The business was closed for the season, but he was happy to give me a quick tour and tell me about the place, including the organic gardens. When I mentioned I was reading *Voices*, he laughed and said that Robert originally had owned the place for more than a decade. He had built the building we were in for a movie set, and also a studio up behind the original house.

That studio was where his book was written. I found this so interesting in a way that usually indicates something is afoot. Later that night I reread Robert's introduction where he talks about learning from nature, the land, and the ancestors, as he lived on Flinders for ten years.

The intro also includes a story about the visit of his Aboriginal friend, Brian. They went to the Wybalenna cemetery and Brian could feel his ancestors were not there. Later one evening, when they walked out behind the house at Healing Dreams to see the sunset — Brian suddenly realized his ancestors were there. Robert later discovered that this was where the Aboriginals from Wybalenna would occasionally come. Where they could view the Tassie mainland — wailing and trying to throw themselves back to their homeland.

As I drove away from Healing Dreams I had one of those "thoughtless thoughts" that come as a knowing. Robert Lawlor was being seeded with information while he lived there — information that eventually came together in the book *Voices*.

There are many things I know that I can't validate, so I'm never quite sure how much to believe them or not. However years later, I would have the chance to meet Robert at Healing Dreams. I asked him directly if he felt as if he had been seeded with information while he lived there. Without hesitation, he said yes, and told me a story of sleeping on the beach and waking to find the Aboriginal spirits dancing around him.

Fotheringate Beach

Many people had recommended going to Trousers Point beach, "one of the most photographed beaches in the world." It was nice, but I had no pull to be there. I stopped for a quick peek, but felt nothing — no rightness, no pull, no thoughtless direction.

So I turned back and headed to Fotheringate Beach instead. It was late afternoon and I was watching in the bush to see if I might spot an echidna or a wombat.

There was no one around, so I could drive as slowly as I wanted. Hoping . . . .

Then I see a big rock suddenly run into a hole. I was so surprised; I was sure that was a rock. So as I kept crawling along, I watched the rocks carefully. Sure enough, another couple of rocks ran for their holes.

I was thrilled to finally see a couple of wombats. *But I'm not sure I can really claim to have seen them,* I thought, laughing. *I did see some running rocks.*

When I got to the Fotheringate car park, although the sign pointed right to the beach, I headed left on the track out to the rocky coast. It was an easy path and took me out onto some of the most amazing rocks I have ever seen. They were immense and very rounded with weird little dents and holes. They reminded me of bodies, and some of the faces looked alien.

View looking west from Trousers Point Coastal Track,
Flinders Island, Tasmania

There was no beach here, just the rocky outcropping being pounded by the crashing waves. I could see so far across the waters. There were a few islands around — and a great view of the distinctive Chapel Island, rumored to have the largest tiger snakes in the world.

I sat there just absorbing the amazing moment: surrounded by mountain, sea, bush, and a waning sun. What a wondrous life! I sat there pouring my gratitude and thoughts into my journal. Every once in a while I would look back at the path. No thought, I would just turn and look. I'm writing away, and suddenly, without a thought, I'm writing . . . *I'm not alone.*

I look again back at the path and don't see anyone, so I continue writing . . . *I'm not alone. There is a male Aboriginal spirit here, sitting beside me.*

I'm surprised, but allow myself to keep writing, curious about what is going to come out. *Does he have something he wants to say to me?* I silently asked.

Yes, he wants you to know you're welcome here. They are glad you came. They appreciate the way you walk on the earth — with reverence. Please help our people.

The Tassie Aboriginals? I asked in writing.

Yes, and more — all of humanity. Help to free them from what makes them so ugly to each other, is the response on paper.

You are the seed of the new being. You are not the fruit — it is not time for you to decay, he continued, making reference to something in Lawlor's book, and answering my unspoken question. I was trying desperately not to repress his words, but to let them come through clearly.

It's time for you to blossom. You can do more than you know. The ancestors will work with you and through you. Do not doubt yourself or them. We have waited a long time for you to be ready. There are others too, coming of age. All of creation is supporting you. The ground is ready — the ground of

consciousness. Your fertile ground is in consciousness. Yes, it's true — be the gardener in consciousness.

Why should I believe this? I asked.

To which he replied, **We gave you wombats.**

Hart had told me that something would happen on Flinders Island, and remembering this now, I silently ask. *What will you change my mind about?*

How difficult you think this will be. What do you want tomorrow? A beautiful shell on the beach? Go at sunrise.

A conch shell springs into my head — and I immediately know which beach.

Then I'm told to go within — and I felt instructions to "mother" my tribe in consciousness. Teach them as Aboriginal children have been taught. Teach them their relations. Help them grow up. Give them the love and attention they didn't get.

The Conch Shell

The island is said to have 120 beaches. I managed to get to about ten of them in the six days I wandered, and they were all beautiful and empty — and surprisingly different. Some had fine sand, others coarse. Sometimes the rocks were rounded, or lacey, or covered in orange lichen. And everywhere, shells were plentiful with an amazing variety, which changed in each location. However, after having walked for hours on these beaches I had not seen any conch-shell fragments at all — so I was a bit skeptical about him being able to fulfill his promise.

The next morning I went out early, straight to Patriarch Inlet. I parked on the sandy road and headed to the beach through the scrub. As soon as I hit the sand, within two feet I found a conch shell the size of my hand. It was so far from the tide line that I couldn't even imagine how it got there. It was a big, clunky one — not quite beautiful, but it was as he promised. I was amazed — astounded to find one intact. *Thank you.*

What do you want tomorrow? A beautiful shell on the beach?
Go at sunrise.

Easier Than You Think

There is so much out there these days about manifesting that has never quite resonated with me. While I do believe we are infinitely more powerful than we know, and also that we do create our reality on some level, I also feel manifesting has been grossly oversimplified. It's been reduced to not much more than the ego trying to get what it desires rather than being willing to be guided or follow a true soul path.

I had been thinking about the message from that spirit on Fotheringate, particularly as it related to moving through life with ease. So I considered his suggestion that I expected things to be more difficult than they needed to be. He was definitely right — while I believed in miracles and grace, I was very sporadic in allowing them to work in my life. I sensed that I needed to turn more "concerns" over to an easier way, probably through asking for help more consistently, even in those areas where it seems impossible. I also needed to work closer to the moment — instead of trying to get big help for something years or months away, I needed to shift my focus to today or tomorrow — to receive help with the day-to-day challenges.

I decided to try these ideas out in my life and see what would happen. So while I walked the beach later that day, I said a little prayer and asked for help.

I'm flying away today, back to Launceston and then have to pick up my heavy pack and walk down the road a kilometer to the main airport. From there I fly to Brisbane, where I'm taking a bus into the City Centre. I've booked a backpackers, but have to cross an eight-lane highway to get there — and I'm arriving at midnight. Is there any way you can help make this day a bit easier? That would be wonderful if you can. Thanks so very much. I didn't know to whom I was addressing this request. I figured they could work it out in the mailroom.

Hours later, as I flew away from Flinders Island, I was aware how deeply I could feel under the sea, and the gentle movement there. I had the most overwhelming feeling that I was the consciousness under the ocean — it felt so natural, like I was breathing the tides. I shifted my focus and realized I could also feel deeply into the earth, or out into the atmosphere, or way out into the galaxy. I could expand my awareness to be all of those as well. But still, I kept returning to the ocean — I AM the consciousness of the ocean.

WOW, that's a new one. Cool, though.

209

As the plane landed, I pulled myself back into reality. The little plane taxied up to the small terminal and stopped. The door opened and a guy stuck his head in.

"Where are those two women that need a ride to the main terminal?" he asked.

"We're here. We have a flight leaving in an hour," they piped up.

"Great, I have a car here. We'll get your bags and I'll drive you down. No worries."

"Hello, is there any way I can get a ride, too?" I quickly asked, not wanting to miss this opportunity.

"No worries, there's room," he replied.

"Fantastic," I chirped. I could barely believe my ears. As they unloaded the people and their luggage, I ran inside and grabbed my heavy pack from storage.

"Too easy," I muttered as I hurried to the car on the tarmac.

When I arrived in Brisbane, I caught the bus with no problems. I was quite weary and not looking forward to a big city bus terminal at midnight. I was also wondering if I'd have to carry my bags up or down stairs to cross the eight-lane highway.

"Looks like you're my last passenger. Are you the going to the downtown terminal?" The bus driver asked as he glanced back.

"Yeah," I responded sleepily.

"I'll bet you're going to one of the backpackers across the street," he guessed.

"Yeah, that's right." I opened my eyes and began paying attention.

"Why don't I just drop you off there so you don't have to lug your bags over the road?" he suggested.

"That would be fantastic," I said happily, "I would be so very grateful."

"Done. No worries," he said, giving me a thumbs-up.

As I crawled into bed that night in a room full of strangers, I marveled at how easy and graceful this day had been. I was in awe at how the perfect help was given — help I could not have imagined or thought up. It was *grace*, flow, allowing myself to be blessed rather than always needing to control or prepare or manage. I was amazed and grateful.

As I drifted off to sleep, I realized — *I feel blessed beyond my wildest dreams.*

Seeded by Creation

"Hey, Hart. I know why you kept getting a 'no' on my going to Flinders Island during most of the trip," I chirped.

"Oh yeah? Why's that?" she asked.

"Well, I think I told you that Robert Lawlor had been seeded with the information for *Voices* while he was living on Flinders. He alluded to it in his book, but I suddenly *knew* it while I was driving around. I had been wondering why Flinders was always a 'no' until the end of week three. And then suddenly it's a nine out of ten."

"Yeah, I wondered that too." Hart replied.

"So the other day I wasn't really thinking about it and the answer popped in. They needed to see if they could seed my mind with information and then have it flow through me onto paper without too much interference. It became a 'yes' just a few days after Creation wrote the twelve pages in my journal — about all the things I was reading, but also calling upon so many other thoughts and information I've encountered in the last few years. They needed to see if I could let it come through. Once I did, then going to Sisters closed down, and Flinders Island became a nine," I suggested.

Hart was quiet for a moment, feeling for the truth of that idea. Finally she spoke. "You know, Sue, I believe you're right on that one."

Wombat, Flinders Island, Tasmania

PART 3
The Aftermath

Chapter 29

What Now?

I'd been back from Australia a month and I was flying to California for the last Mystery School of the year. I was still integrating all that had happened on my trip. Frequently, I noticed a question floating through my mind . . . **What happened on Flinders Island?**

I knew something momentous had happened there but I couldn't put my finger on it. I had been in Tassie four weeks and was incredibly happy the whole time, but it wasn't until Flinders that I began noticing an amazing internal spaciousness. I could still worry and doubt on a surface level, but this new quality was untouched. It felt so expansive and yet content in the moment. As I looked out the plane's window at the circular rainbows in the clouds, I got a deep sense — the kind of deep sense I usually ignore or forget — that I would need to write a book about this adventure.

Two things happened at that Mystery School that were pivotal. At dinner the first night, I shared my adventure with about a dozen people. It was the first time I had spoken about what had happened with anyone but Hart. But I knew these people by now, and knew I could be honest with them.

I was truly stunned by how they embraced my story. They were excited and immediately started talking about me needing to write a book.

They were so very enthusiastic and met my uncertainty with their certainty. Maria an award winning writer, even gave me ideas on easy ways to record the story and have it transcribed. I was blown away, yet buoyed with optimism. I was getting resounding encouragement for what I had known. How could I ignore it now?

The other question everyone had . . . What now?

The silence within me was deafening.

I had no idea what now. I'd go spend the holidays with my folks, and then come back to Oregon and get my RV out of storage. And try to figure out where I could go to find the sweetness in life.

Fortunately a conversation with Julia, Jean's office manager, solved the "what next" dilemma. At the end of the Social Artistry program, we had talked about me working there, but I knew it couldn't happen before I went to Tassie. Now that I was back, she was still interested.

I began planning to move to Ashland, Oregon — where my people were. It was amazing to remember four years earlier when an accounting client in Massachusetts was introducing me to his visiting daughter. She immediately blurted, "Ashland, Oregon. If you go to Ashland, Oregon, you'll find your people." She paused and then said, "Oops, sorry. Sometimes I get random things about people and it just pops out."

"Not a problem. Thanks for sharing it," I had responded, not knowing how right she would be.

Integration

The next six months were definitely a time of integration. I settled into a sweet little cottage in Ashland and began working in Jean's office. It was less money than accounting, but not as soul-numbing, so I was happy to make the change. This meant I was staff at the following year's Mystery School, which was great.

Gradually, as it all began to integrate, I started to realize "things" about my trip. Sometimes un-thought thoughts would just surface in my mind with a particularly interesting feel to them, so I would know it wasn't just me thinking.

For example, in the kitchen one day I was asking myself for the hundredth time, "What the hell happened on Flinders Island?" Suddenly I *knew*. That first night on Walker's Lookout, it wasn't another group Aboriginal consciousness. It was totally different. Why hadn't that occurred to me? I must have recognized something because I didn't try to break agreements with them. I *knew* that I had met the Galactic Formulating Consciousness of the Earth and its inhabitants. I could feel the rightness, and later that day Hart agreed.

Other revelations came through conversations with Hart or others . . . .

"I still do the gyrating infinity symbol, but new locations keep being added," I shared with Hart one day.

"Oh yeah? Like where?" she queried.

"Well, besides the center of my head, and my heart, it now also hits my throat, the first three chakras, but then it goes to my knees, my feet and a couple of locations lower than my feet down into the earth."

"Oh, yeah, I've heard there are chakras there," she offered.

"But it also goes to my crown and to about five spots above my crown. They all get gyrating at once. It's a real trip." I smiled thinking about it.

"Okay, Sue, why don't you do it now and let me see what's happening?" Hart suggested.

"Oh, great idea. Okay. Just gimme me a sec." I put down my tea and closed my eyes. I was standing in the kitchen, and activated the first infinity symbol in the center of my head.

"Okay, I've started the first one. They continue on from there in the order that suits them. It's never in a straight line — it always jumps around a bit," I said quietly while focusing on the internal gymnastics.

"That's really interesting Sue," Hart said thoughtfully. "It's like the whole thing wants to turn inside out. Have you ever tried that?"

"Well, no, not really," I paused as I focused in again, "but I can try it now. Oh my god, it flips really easily."

"How does that feel, Sue?"

"It feels great. Like going beyond here and now," I said. "WOW!"

"Sue, it's like a wormhole. That's amazing," Hart exclaimed as she watched the energetics of me and my wormhole from the other side of the country.

I Can't Do That!

As the months went by, life was great. I still wasn't wildly healthy, I still was maxed on my credit cards, but I felt like I was in the right place. I may not be doing what I ultimately was here to do — but at least I was heading in the right direction. I knew I was on a wave and it was going somewhere. It was so much more fun than being dead in the water. I had experienced that feeling for way too long after my illness. I hoped never to be in that place again.

So I kept watching for signs, waiting for cues or directions, and kept talking to Hart.

"Sue, you definitely have a book to write. But you're not going to be able to write it where you are." Hart's comment sent a bit of a shudder through my being.

"Really? Where do I have to be?" I asked, slightly annoyed.

She paused and something told me I wasn't going to like the answer.

"You need to go back to Flinders Island. You need to write your book there," she offered quietly.

"I can't do that!" My lament was so familiar. Seems I said the same thing just nine months earlier. "My cards are maxed and I don't have the money to do that. And I don't have vacation pay to get me there this time," I continued in protest.

"Well, just sit with it, Sue, and see what presents itself," Hart offered kindly. She and I both knew that my usual knee-jerk reaction to Spirit's calling was a "no," followed closely by a "maybe," and ultimately a "yes!"

I was grumbling at the thought, then started to come around. "How long do I need to go for?" I asked, figuring I may as well get some specifics so I know what I'm up against.

"It looks like six months to me," she said with a little laugh, knowing I was about to groan.

"How can I possibly go for six months?" I whined quietly. "Why do I have to go there?"

Hart paused again before answering. "There's something there that wants to connect with you. It's probably this galactic consciousness you talk about. It feels like you need to be in its energy for this to emerge."

Obviously we both thought she was talking about the book emerging. Little did we know.

I smiled, Spirit always knew how to entice me into the next adventure. "All right, I'll think about it."

I already had experience with impossible things transpiring, especially when I originally quit accounting full time. I had spent four years living in *grace* and traveling, all with no visible means of support. I had maxed and paid off my credit cards at least four times in that period. Certainly this couldn't be any harder than that.

"Sue, you are able to manifest things better than anyone I know. After all you've been through, this should be a piece of cake," she encouraged me in her matter-of-fact way.

"Yeah, I know," I said quietly, "but the Universe is going to have to show me how."

Undeniable Signs

One Saturday morning, while languishing in bed, it occurred to me that I needed absolute guidance about this.

If I'm meant to return to Tasmania, you need to give me a sign, and make it so frigging clear that I can't miss it, was my silent request. I was a bit defiant, but I loved my little cottage, I was meeting wonderful people, and the work was okay. Did I have to uproot myself again and live on the edge for six months?

You know I'll do whatever I'm meant to do, but you need to tell me directly, and not through someone else.

I had used this "give me a sign" process when I was in Nepal and woke up one morning knowing I was meant to go to

New Zealand. I was shocked when the sign showed up hours later, so I tried it again a few days later, and again the answer was clear. Most quandaries weren't important enough to bother with, but this time I needed an answer.

And again the swiftness of the response was staggering. Two hours later I stopped into the little consignment shop in Ashland. There were only three people in the shop — the clerk and two customers trying on clothes. While I waited for a dressing room, I could hear them talking.

"So what's going on with your daughter? She was going to have a year away last I heard. Did she go?" asked one woman.

"Yeah, Cindy is taking a year at the University in Melbourne. She's absolutely loving it," offered the proud mom. "She called the other day, and this weekend she's gone with a group to visit *Tasmania*."

The world stood still as that soaked into my brain. No one ever talks about Tasmania. Most people have no idea where it is or that it even exists. They keep thinking I'm talking about Tanzania.

I was stunned as I wandered out into the sunshine. I could feel the other dimensions — plotting my future.

"All right," I mutter to myself, "How am I going to do this?"

The next day I was talking to a Mystery School friend and explaining my dilemma. She told me about when she was trying to get to India to meet the family of her fiancé and didn't have the money. She just kept telling people she was going even though she didn't know how. And by the time she was meant to leave, it was all taken care of. I thought it was a great idea, but I was unsure it would work for me. I had no untapped resources to make this happen, but I was willing to give it a go.

A few weeks earlier, I had signed up for a webinar series with Oprah and Eckhart Tolle. It wasn't something I'd normally have done, but when the email came the day before it started I just signed up without thinking. I remembered the very first episode, when they were saying they had half a million people signed up. I was in awe, and my first thought was, *Oh my God, the world is never going to be the same again.*

So Monday night, two days after the consignment shop, I was sitting down to watch the third or fourth episode of the ten-part webinar.

Oprah and Eckhart were there, and Oprah was doing the intro. After welcoming Eckhart, she turned to her piece of paper and started welcoming the world . . . "We have people online from China, Russia, Lithuania, and . . ." her voice dropped as she stumbled, "Tas, Tas, Tas, Tasmania." Then she looked straight into the camera and gleefully shouted, "HELLO TASMANIA!"

I sat there positively stunned. I couldn't hear another word. I was flabbergasted.

All right! I'll go, I said quietly to myself and them. *I'll go. Help me figure out how.*

From then on I started acting as if I was going. I wrote to Gerard from the cabin park and David from Healing Dreams asking if they knew of any affordable accommodation for six months. Before they could even respond I knew I was meant to stay on the Healing Dreams property, so I wrote the owners directly and introduced myself. Funny thing — when Gerard and David responded, they both recommended Healing Dreams. Apparently all roads really do lead to this place.

After a few emails and a phone call, and some pictures of possible places to stay on their property, we finally settled on my renting the studio out back — the place where *Voices* was written. This book had been so pivotal in my experience, and I would be staying on the property where Robert had been seeded with information. I was amazed and grateful and knew it was right.

I started to tell people I was going to go back, without naming a time. At work I knew I had done what I'd come for and that I was finished there. I let them know that I would be leaving and would give them whatever time they needed to replace me.

Miracle from Dad

I was on my way to visit my folks, and as always, my dad was picking me up. We had a ritual of going for Mexican food on the way home from the airport. This was when we had some quiet time together to talk about things. I had learned long ago that to have a decent relationship with my dad, I would have to make good use of the time we had alone, because my mom tended to monopolize every conversation.

Twenty years earlier, when I had quit my accounting job, he and I went on a week's trip to Montana and Glacier National Park. We were at lunch, catching up, talking about my unemployed status and what I planned to do next. The conversation was a shock to me because I could see that my dad didn't really know me. But I also realized that I hadn't really given him the chance to know me. I decided then to start being more forthright with him about the things I was doing and what was important to me.

So as I began my spiritual journey I vaguely would fill him in on what was going on with me. I was gentle and not overly honest, but felt it was important for him to be allowed to see the real me. Funny thing is, the more straightforward I was with him, the more accepting he was. It's almost as if he could feel what was real in me. My dad had been a brilliant civil engineer, so my spiritual leanings were quite a foreign language to him.

Yet when I returned from Tassie, I had been honest about my mystical experiences. My dad was obviously very intrigued and even mentioned how much he had enjoyed the email updates I'd sent to everyone, even though he often didn't understand what I was talking about.

So during our burritos and enchiladas, I told him about the book. I told him about the response from the Mystery School bunch. And I told him I would need to return to Flinders for six months to do the writing. I explained my financial situation and asked if I could borrow some money to make this trip. He was quite happy to say yes.

It wasn't the way I would have liked to have funded this trip, but I was committed to the journey. If they could make Oprah yell TASMANIA into the camera while I was online watching, it must be important for me to go.

A few days later, I saw him looking through a New Age book catalog my mom had.

"What are you looking for?" I asked him, surprised to see him with it.

Embarrassed at being caught, he said, "I'm just looking to see where your book will fit in."

That simple moment spoke volumes and was a great encouragement to me. I *knew* I was indeed heading in the right direction.

How Did That Happen?

The next hurdle was a visa for Australia for six months. They require things like proof of financial means — something that I was obviously weak on. Things like copies of bank statements and pay stubs or whatever. As I filled out the forms online, I was honest but I was definitely nervous because my bank statements were not impressive.

When I'd finished the main application I went to start scanning and adding in my bank statements. Something weird happened and suddenly the application had been filed.

"Wait! I haven't added my bank statements," I yelled at the computer.

I quickly signed back in to the immigration website to see how to go about adding the required documents.

"Oh, my god. How did that happen?" I muttered. I was stunned.

Another of those moments when you can feel the divine setup, your destiny barreling toward you. I sat there staring at the screen wondering how they approved me without required documentation. And for a whole *year.*

What are you setting me up for now? I smell a plan that I don't know about.

Epilogue

I knew 20 years ago that I was here to somehow help humanity move through this quantum leap we are all facing. I could feel it in every fiber of my being, even though I didn't know what it would look like or how I could help. So many steps along the path appeared strange or unusual to me, yet all were necessary for me to find my way. The most potent steps?

- Breaking the agreement with the other soul group to engage in torture was a moment of divine intervention that has grown exponentially in its potential application.
- Receiving twelve pages in my journal — a message from Creation that unlocked my mind, freed my knowing, and prompted me to ask outrageous questions that push the boundaries of what we believe is possible. Seeds were sown that night and left to sprout, providing a new foundation within me that years later would gradually answer these

questions — about humanity and what was possible. What would it take for us to evolve beyond the negative fear-based paradigm?

- Recognizing the magnitude of that meeting on Walkers Lookout that first night on Flinders. And gradually, gently, fluidly, allowing the Galactic Formulating Consciousness to surround me with grace, enfold me in their wisdom, and enable me to embrace the path before me. It was through their guidance and continued support that I would eventually birth a protocol that unravels the —Why? And what can I do to help? (See Afterword for more on this protocol – the Wholeness Alignment Process)

What transpired from this trip to Tasmania — this missing piece — I would never have imagined or seen coming. Yet it's amazing to look back on my life and see how all events, all side tracks, all stumbles, were preparing me for now — to be me, and to fulfill my purpose.

As with so many people I've talked to, I always felt like I wasn't on the right track. I eventually discovered that I wasn't lost, I was just in training. Now at least I have an inkling of the path I'm following, but I'm still in training, still being guided and led to the next step. But it's so much more fun knowing I'm on a real path — *my* path.

For years people have told me how courageous I was to do some of the things I have done. In my heart, I knew it wasn't really courage. It's a strange combination of avoidance and trust. I hated the idea of being a plastic ukulele my whole life — of plodding along in a meaningless existence. I definitely wanted to avoid as many 2x4's as I could. And I somehow had a deep trust of something beyond what I could see, feel, or know.

We're all afraid — of change, of the unknown, and of getting out of our comfort zone. Fear isn't the problem. You're going to feel it. But letting it dictate your choices and actions — letting it keep you small — letting it keep you from being fully alive — that's the real issue. Fear of fear dictating my life is what propelled me into courage. Looking back, there were so many times I was afraid, and yet in the overcoming of fear came freedom, empowerment — and *Life*.

To this day I'm still moving on an unfolding path, I'm still becoming, not completely certain where it all leads. But I feel the changes coming and my arms are open wide. There's something emerging in me as it's emerging in you, and I can't wait to meet us. We are like a field of wildflowers, all different, all beautiful, all blooming to our own destiny. We're each unique, with so much to give the world and each other. I revel in our diversity — I love watching us bloom, blossom, and flourish as we grow in certainty about who we really are and why.

I share my story to encourage and remind you — that you are encoded like a seed — designed perfectly to fulfill your life's purpose. Is it possible you are already on your path or perhaps in training? Just trust it, embrace it, and appreciate yourself.

I encourage each of you to find the courage within to audaciously be your most authentic self. To fulfill the mission that you designed for yourself, to be blessed with whatever miracles you most need. And to open up and receive all the help you need in this moment and every moment.

The Ancient Ones are calling us. The message I was given on Flinders Island is for all of us. Please remember...

"You are the seed of the new being. You are not the fruit — it is not time for you to decay — it's time for you to blossom. You can do more than you know. The ancestors will work with you and through you. Do not doubt yourself or them. We have waited a long time for you to be ready. There are others too, coming of age. All of Creation is supporting you. The ground is ready — the ground of consciousness. Your fertile ground is in consciousness – be the gardener in consciousness."

— **The Ancient Ones**

Afterword

As you can see, by the end of this book I was becoming confident in my knowing, but I still was not fully embracing my gifts and trusting myself.

I returned to Flinders Island and continued to deepen my connection with the consciousness that had called me there. Through Lyme disease, a failed marriage, and other challenges, I trusted Spirit and followed my inner knowing along the path laid before me. I realized I was in training, and finally recognized how I was to assist myself and others into embracing our Wholeness.

The **Wholeness Alignment Process** emerged from this training – landing in my lap in a three week period. This Spirit guided protocol changed everything, and my life has never the same.

My Lyme disease was completely cleared and I regained better health than I had ever experienced in my life. But the most amazing gift of the **Wholeness Alignment Process**, was the radical change into full alignment with my Divine Self. I quickly experienced a sense of Wholeness and the heightened ability to listen and follow my life's purpose.

Since 2014, I have been utilizing the **Wholeness Alignment Process** to help others who are feeling the "calling" to their soul's purpose, but are being blocked by numerous things including illness, interference, past life "bleed through", and more. The Circle of Consciousness continues to work with me with clients, guiding and fine tuning the development of this ground breaking work.

Wholeness Alignment Process (WAP)

The **Wholeness Alignment Process** (Previously known as the Whole Being Alignment) is a life changing protocol that enables you to make a quantum leap into vibrant Wholeness – activating and empowering you by:

- Enabling you to fully restore your soul's alignment with your Divine Self, your Essence, the highest you.
- Empowering you to move forward with ease and *grace.*
- Clearing subconscious blocks to your Wholeness, such as interference, unconscious programming or patterning, and excess emotional baggage.
- Breaking those karmic or soul agreements that are causing you suffering or keeping you stuck in old patterns, including ancestral ones.
- Realigning and resetting your body for optimal health.
- Releasing deeply embedded trauma carried for lifetimes.
- Facilitating your ability to make breakthroughs in your life, your health, and your purpose.

If you are ready to make a quantum leap into your Wholeness, free of the blocks and baggage, then go to my website for more information. You can sign up on the website to receive a free gift designed to accelerate this process in you, and also to be notified of new videos, blogs, and programs.

www.SueCimino.com
Facebook – Sue Cimino – Author
Facebook – Wholeness Alignment Process

Creation's Message – The next book includes a special gift for YOU!

Ancient Ones Are Calling Us was the just the beginning of an amazing journey. I did return to Flinders Island and Creation continued to "seed" me with awareness, ideas, and information.

Creation's Message will go into much more depth about the Galactic Formulating Consciousness and what it wants you to know. You will journey with me through the revelations and challenges, including the discovery of how Lyme disease was the catalyst to receiving the **Wholeness Alignment Process**.

The goal of this next book and my work with Creation is to enable you to fully embrace YOUR Wholeness. *Creation's Message* is designed to activate you so that you, the reader, are able to access the **Wholeness Alignment Process** directly – for free – and move into the life that has been calling you. A life that is fulfilling, graceful, and empowers you to reach your highest potential.

Creation's Message will be coming out in 2018. To receive updates and news of its release, sign up on my website or my author page:

www.SueCimino.com
Facebook – Sue Cimino – Author
Facebook – Wholeness Alignment Process

Acknowledgements

I am eternally grateful to the Ancient Ones for calling me to Tasmania, connecting with me on Flinders Island and guiding me along this convoluted path to fulfill my life's purpose. I am deeply humbled by this journey and blown away by what is possible. Words can never express my delight and gratefulness.

My utmost gratitude goes to the islands of Tasmania and to all the indigenous spirits and group consciousness who are connected to that land. Thanks for preserving that clear, crisp, wildness and for being what you are. I will forever be deeply touched.

Thanks to my dad, Robert Vanderlyn, for believing in me through the years in spite of the strangeness of my journey. You changed my life when you took the family camping across the USA for a month in 1968. I discovered there was a whole world out there and my free spirited soul hasn't settled since.

I also need to thank all the 'seers' for helping me along my way until I learned to listen and know for myself. Their input and validation enabled me to jump off more than a few cliffs as I followed my destiny. For this book I need to specifically mention . . .

- Hart Brent did what I was unable to – seeing beyond my "rock-ness" to the real me, and then articulating that in words I could recognize. That was absolutely life changing. Answering of all my questions with such clarity and integrity allowed me to grow into my own knowing and eventually trust myself. Giving me back my health twenty years earlier was fantastic too.

- Karen Langley creatively and lovingly helped me through three of my roughest years – my dark night of the soul – with her spiritual counseling and sessions. It was through one of these regressions that I accidently recognized the possibility of breaking agreements.

After nine years marinating in *A Course in Miracles* in the '90s, it's in every fiber of my being and has given me an unshakeable foundation in the benevolent Universe that we live in. From this sprang the revelation about our ability to go beyond forgiveness to breaking agreements and freeing both sides. I will be forever grateful.

The 2007 West Coast Mystery School played an enormous role in setting me off on this journey. So many participants were inspiring and encouraging, but I must single out a few. . .

- Jean Houston made my head spin with possibilities and inspiration. The processes that she offered gave me a context to unleash the greater me, and helped me invite more of myself into my being. Tasmania absolutely turned out to be fertile ground, and so I believe 'the gifting' worked!
- Deep gratitude to Margot Cairnes for doing the future regression and discovering there was a missing piece.
- I'm particularly grateful to that table of twelve at the December weekend who listened to my story and popped the "write a book?" question. It was everyone's enthusiastic support that made me realize this book was a real possibility. I have carried that memory with me for the last 10 years. Thanks.

My deepest thanks to Tom Bird for fulfilling his life's mission and offering his writing retreats to the world. Without his method, guidance, and support, this book would still be languishing within and waiting to be born. Thanks also to Tom Bird's Publish Now team – especially Sabrina Fritts and John Hodgkinson.

Thanks also to Kathy Mason and Denise Cassino for your encouragement, marketing expertise, and for helping me with more than you needed to.

Thanks to my first readers for their feedback and encouragement: Gudrun Steffen, Shulé Marie Besher, Tracey Lescalleet and Robert Vanderlyn.

I especially thank Jill Maynard for her input regarding the Tasmanian Aboriginal history, and for catching my errors.

And special thanks go to Dave Freer and the Flinders Island Writing Group for pushing me beyond my comfort zone and teaching me so much. Dave, you were the one who helped me to appreciate my voice, giving me the courage to finally write and share. That was a vital piece of this puzzle.

But the biggest thanks go to you, the reader. Without you out there waiting for this, there would have been no reason.

Contacts

Hart Brent – The amazing Hart that I talked with throughout the book has an office in Florence, MA and Peacham, VT. I highly recommend her for health issues and so much more. Generally she only works in person.

https://www.healthcallsus.net/ - Hart "has 28 years of experience promoting self health care: advocating for client's whole health, perceived as 50% physical (biochemical) & 50% subtle (emotional, mental, spiritual)." She ". . . . Provides a balanced protocol designed just for you that may include: homeopathy, herbs, essential oils, supplements, diet and lifestyle suggestions so that your vitality will be supported 100%."

Healing Dreams has been renamed Mountain Seas Art and Wilderness Retreat - www.mountainseas.com.au

About the Author

Sue is an author, speaker, gifted intuitive, visionary, and a believer in miracles. After a spiritual awakening in 1986, Sue quit her CPA accounting job to follow Spirit. She began traveling extensively, looking for the truth, and for her purpose. Sue spent 9 years immersed in A Course In Miracles, which laid a deep foundation of what's true, real, and possible.

Because of lifelong health issues, she studied multiple healing modalities, most recently training with Marisa Peer in Rapid Transformational Therapy and is certified as an MPM Hypnotherapist. She also trained as a BICOM Bioresonance Therapist.

Sue was called to Tasmania in 2007 where she began receiving messages from Creation about what's going on with humanity and how we can be helped. In 2014, Sue received the

Wholeness Alignment Process, a life changing protocol designed to help people align with their Divine Self.

Sue has been assisting people around the world to remember and embrace their innate Wholeness, through sessions and programs, both in person and online. She is passionate about empowering people to reach their full potential and bring their unique gifts to the world. She is also passionate about bright colors, cats, deep conversations, and nature.

You can sign up on the website to receive a free gift designed to accelerate the process of Wholeness in you, and also to be notified of new videos, blogs, and programs.

www.SueCimino.com

Facebook – Sue Cimino – Author

Facebook – Wholeness Alignment Process

Feeling Inspired? What now?

- Sign up on the website to receive a free gift designed to accelerate the process of Wholeness in you. You will also be notified of new videos, blogs, and programs.

www.SueCimino.com

- Like the following Facebook pages to interact with others who are experiencing this emerging Wholeness, and to hear of news and offerings.

Facebook – Sue Cimino – Author
Facebook – Wholeness Alignment Process

- Share this book and information with your friends and family who would be interested.

- Leave a review on Amazon, Goodreads, or any other literary review website.

- Request this book at your local bookstore.

THANK YOU!